BORN & BREAD

ROBERT SWIFT

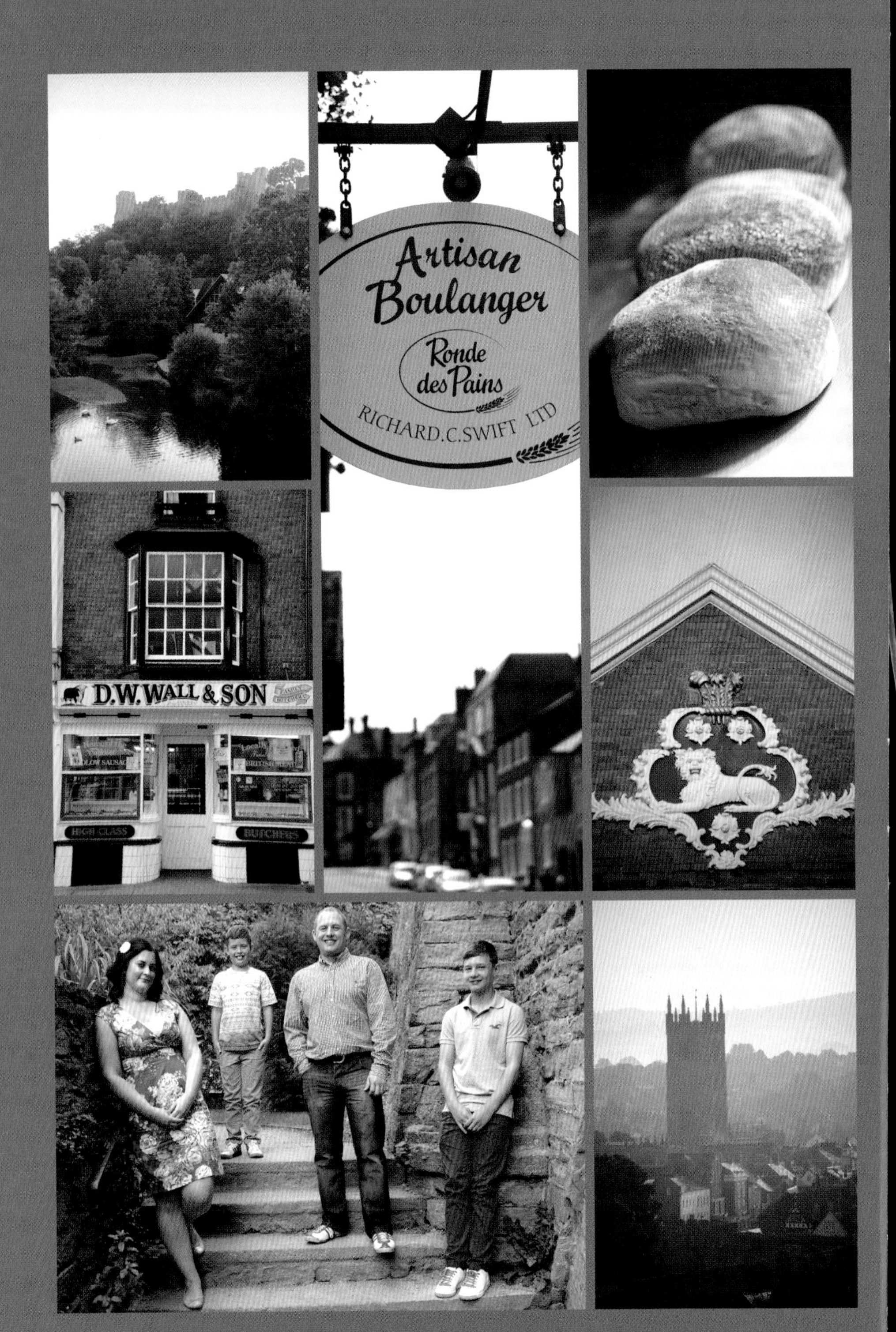
Artisan
Boulanger
Ronde
des Pains
RICHARD.C.SWIFT LTD
D.W. WALL & SON
HIGH CLASS
BUTCHERS

FEATHERS
HOTEL

For my darling
LUCI
and six generations of the
Swift family

First published in Great Britain in 2013 by
www.awaywithmedia.com,
Shrewsbury SY3 7LN

ISBN: 978-0-9576292-2-6

Edited, photographed and published by
Andrew Richardson

Editorial production
Adam Haynes

FOREWORD

WHEN Rob asked me to write the foreword for his first book I had no problem in saying yes.

The first time I heard about Rob's bread was when I was asked to demonstrate at Ludlow Food Festival. I managed to catch one of his interactive demos, for which he got the crowd involved in making and kneading the bread. Once I'd seen his demo I went off in search of his stall, so that I could buy some of his produce.

After getting the selection of breads home, we sampled them with local butter, cheeses and chutney. The texture of those loaves was really good. They had been perfectly proved and kneaded, with just the write amount of seasoning. I was very impressed.

Over the years I saw Rob at a number of local and national food festivals where we were both presenting demonstrations. I always made sure I got a few of his breads before I headed home.

In December 2013 my wife, Jenny, and I purchased Brompton Cookery School, just outside Shrewsbury. It's in a fantastic location and provides a perfect atmosphere for teaching. As soon as we starting discussing courses, Jenny and I had no doubt that we wanted Rob to take all our bread courses. His knowledge of bread is fantastic, both his personality and his teaching style are relaxed, and his courses are friendly and informative.

MARCUS BEAN
Chef and proprietor of Brompton Cookery School

I'm sure Rob has yeast running through his veins, and I love the fact that Rob's family has been baking bread for 150 years; it makes his bakes even more special.

When you try his recipes and follow his tips to get the perfect bake you will not be disappointed.

I know that Rob will be passing down his knowledge and skill to his children, keeping the family trade running in preparation for another 150 years.

Make sure you use this book well. Then pass it on to the next generation. Every family should be able to make great bread and there is no better person than Rob to teach you.

MARCUS BEAN

Robert Swift at his Corve Street bakery.

INTRODUCTION

BEFORE I started to write my first book I asked myself a very simple question: Why Am I Doing This?

In my mind, it was important to understand the reasons for committing these words and pictures to print. The answer I came up with was just as simple: To Try To Help.

I'm passionate about helping home bakers in their quest to create better bread. That's what independent bakers in market towns care about. We make our bread with love, skill, passion and creativity. We give bread a life and we nurture it.

Bread is not an also-ran or a loss-leader that draws people into supermarkets like bears at a honeypot. It's not something that should simply be toasted or turned into a sandwich.

Good artisan bread is a labour of love. It carries a little bit of love in every loaf. It can be enjoyed in many settings, on a variety of occasions, and throughout the seasons.

In recent years, bread has been viewed as a commodity. It's been a product that is considered white, sliced and stuffed in a bag. My family and I consider that sacrilege. We've worked for five generations across 150 years to deliver artisan bread to locals.

I'm committed to making the best bread possible. Bread is versatile and amazing. It has been a staple food for more than 2,000 years and I think we ought to shout about it from the rooftops.

So why am I writing my first book? To help you to bake better bread. I want you to understand the mysteries of a perfect bake. So come on, let's get baking.

ROBERT SWIFT

Contents

Above: Hannah Swift poses outside her grocery store at Wheaton Aston in the second half of the 19th century. *Below*: Progress is evident as Swift deliveries got even swifter.

The Swift Story

IT all began in 1863. Hannah Swift, the great-great-great aunt of Robert Swift, opened a small business in the Staffordshire village of Wheaton Aston. Little could she have imagined that five generations and 150 years later her enterprise would continue to prosper.

Swifts' Bakery has survived two World Wars, economic depression, a technological revolution and, of course, the introduction of the sliced loaf. In fact, not only has Hannah's business made it to the 21st century, it has done so in style. Members of the Swift family continue to innovate and their business is flourishing.

Some things remain the same, however. The 21st-century Swifts' Bakery runs on parallel lines to the 19th-century version. Robert rises early each day to prepare the day's bake, just as Hannah did. His breads are made with the same five basic ingredients that Hannah used: flour, water, salt, yeast *and love*. The family is justifiably proud of its heritage. Its passion for bread is reflected in the high quality of each individually made loaf.

Hannah was a pioneer and she soon introduced her daughter, Harriet, to the business. Harriet brought a third generation into Swifts', in the form of her of nephew Tom, who took over the bakery at the age of 19, having served apprenticeships at bakeries in West Bromwich and Stafford.

Tom produced seven children, one of whom was Charles, a fourth-generation baker. Charles was a fascinating character who continued the baking tradition with his older brother, Walter. Charles worked

Top: Robert's Granddad Charles marries Mary. He got leave from the army for a few days, got married, and returned to regiment.
Above: Charles Swift's book of wartime reminiscences.

"The 21st-century Swifts' Bakery runs on parallel lines to the 19th-century version. The family is justifiably proud of its heritage. Its passion for bread is reflected in the high quality of each individually made loaf."

in the bakery with Tom before being called up to serve in World War II from 1941 to 1946. He was separated from his beloved wife, Mary, but continued to serve in field bakeries during the war, based in Mombasa, east Africa.

When he was demobbed, the partnership with Walter was dissolved. Another brother, also named Tom, had a bakery at Penn, in Wolverhampton, and Charles and Mary took that lease. Their second child, Richard, was to keep the family tradition going.

Charles was ambitious and he founded a new business at Gnosall, in Staffordshire. He worked hard with Mary to build the business and they became a popular couple. Deliveries were difficult, and during winter, so that his regulars received his bread, Charles would battle through snowdrifts that had cut off many outlying areas.

Charles wrote about his experiences in a small booklet, *My Wartime Experiences*, which reflected on his life from 1941 onwards. He recalled: "There were no freezers in those days, so regular deliveries were essential. At Christmas time the village people would bring their turkeys and geese to me on Christmas Day so that they could be cooked in the bakehouse ovens – they were always cooked to perfection.

Charles was passionate about good food and grew his vegetables, as well as making pork pies, cakes and more besides. His son, Richard, worked hard to build upon his parents' work.

Richard had been born in Gnosall, and after serving an apprenticeship and attending Birmingham College of Food and Technology, he became bakery manager.

Richard said: "Jam came in big tins then, not plastic buckets, and I'd stand on the tins so that I could reach the table. I would get up before school and help my father. He'd be baking bread or frying doughnuts and I'd help him out.

"My dad employed three chaps and I started to work there properly during the school holidays. I'd work in the bakery and then go out on the rounds with the delivery drivers. Christmas time was always busy: we'd jelly the pork pies when they were baked."

Richard's diploma in bread, flour and confectionery gave him the knowledge he needed to make a start, and he spent 10 years with his father at Gnosall before striking out. He moved to Clee Hill, in Shropshire, and built a new business from scratch. "That's always been the story in our family. My father left his dad to set up by himself. I left my father and set up by myself. My two sons have also come up with new ideas so that they can make their own mark."

Richard was 29 when he started baking at Clee Hill. "It was owned by two brothers but it was very run down. It had burned down in 1935 and been rebuilt, but it hadn't changed much since then."

Richard and his wife Margaret went about their task with gusto. Their business grew on their joint efforts: Richard would spend long hours in the bakery while Margaret would work out totals, drive vans, keep the company's books up to date and more besides. For both, it was a labour of love.

Richard said: "When I first moved here, I focused on bread. I used to get up and do door-to-door deliveries. I had a little shop on Clee Hill, at the front of the bakery. I'd start at 3.30am then I'd be on the road by 9am. It would be at least 12 hours every day.

"The range was pretty straightforward, with a white loaf and wholemeal. We had very little equipment, just three tables, a place to mix the dough and coke-fired ovens."

The coke-fired ovens did not last. Though they produced an exceptional bake, they were dirty to use. Richard would have to carry coke into the bakery, to fire them. In those early days, he brought in a tonne of flour each week. Today the figure is three tonnes.

He invested in modern equipment, replacing the coke ovens with newer ones. "We extended the bakery in 1984, so that we could make room for oil-fired ovens. That was our first major change. The ovens came from Germany and they worked like a dream. We also invested in big retarder-provers, which are like walk-in fridges. They would slowly warm up through the night and helped us to control the speed at which the dough developed.

"When we arrived for work in the morning, the dough would be ready and we could bake it off."

The refurbishment of the Clee Hill bakery helped to generate additional capacity, so Richard went in search of new business. Having started with one secondhand van and one small shop, he created a business with four shops, three vans and 60 wholesale clients.

Baking became a way of life, rather than just a job.

"The longer it goes on, the earlier it gets. More and more people want good bread. It's a vocation. Now, I can be up at any time from 9pm the night before. I always say 'I've got the bread in me!'. It's a way of life, and a way of life that we all share."

The Clee Hill premises are extended.

"It might seem daft, but we all get a real kick out of making a great loaf and seeing it come out of the oven looking really nice. There is a tremendous amount of satisfaction when it goes well – and terrible frustration when it does not. It's a vocation that has tremendous highs and tremendous lows. In many ways, it's a bit like being an artist."

Richard introduced his two sons, Robert and John, to the business. Like their predecessors, they began at an early age.

John said: "As a boy, I was surrounded by the bakery and, in all fairness, I didn't see myself carrying on the tradition. I always saw it as a tough life. As a teenager, I'd agree to help my dad, but I used to struggle to get up in the mornings.

"There were plenty of times when dad had to wake me by pouring a cup of cold

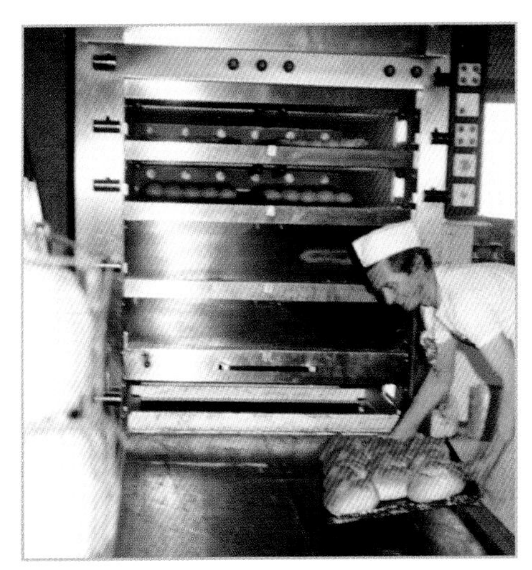
Richard Swift baking at Clee Hill.

water on my face," before he headed off to school. "I was constantly being told off by my teachers for being tired."

On the day he left school, he started working in the bakery. "I was 16. I think my passion for baking really kicked in when I was 24 and married Jayne. I started to take it very seriously then."

"When I was growing up, I'd spent a lot of time with my grandfather, Charles. He was my inspiration. He liked a drink and he liked to do things his own way: I identified with him very strongly.

"The last 30 years have been very exciting, but the next 30 will be even more so. There's something special about being a baker. There are days when we come into the bakery and it's beautifully peaceful. We work on the dough and bake; nothing could be simpler. I'm very proud to be continuing the Swift tradition. My father taught Robert and I everything we know. And, our grandfather was a great inspiration to us too."

Like his forebears, Robert has brought new innovations to the Swift family line. Not content to simply rest on his laurels, he's developed new additions to the Swift family concern. He works in a new bakery in Ludlow's Corve Street and has developed a new company called Bread2Bake along with his wife Lucinda; it provides baking masterclasses and services an ever-growing number of farmers' markets, food festivals and other shows with demonstrations.

Collectively, the Swift family now owns shops in Clee Hill, Craven Arms, Tenbury Wells and Ludlow, and supplies towns such as Cleobury Mortimer, Bewdley, Church Stretton, Clun, Kington and Pembridge.

The family can regularly be found at farmers' markets in Ludlow, Ironbridge, Bewdley and Malvern, as well as at food festivals in Ludlow, Shrewsbury, Shobdon, Tenbury Wells, Builth Wells, Warwick, Stratford-upon-Avon and other parts of the Midlands.

Robert said: "Our bread goes further and further each year, but we're proud of our roots. We work closely with the local community and get involved in talks and demonstrations for local primary and secondary schools, as well as other clubs and societies. We've involved in a project called Skill Builders, which passes on traditional skills to a new generation. Skill Builders is a volunteer-run organisation that works with local schools to connect youngsters to artisan occupations. Hopefully, we're helping the next generation of bakers so that there will still be high-street bakers in another 150 years."

Richard and his two sons take a great pride in their work.

John, Richard and Robert Swift, Ludlow, 2013.

Richard said: "I think the beauty of being part of a small bakery is that we connect with local people every single day. We can be flexible: when a customer asks us for a new type of loaf, we are able to make it. We can create a new line to use seasonal produce. Bigger bakeries can't do that. We are also in touch with our customers. They give us their daily feedback, so we know what they think."

Robert added: "The Swift family has continued to evolve. My grandfather, Charles, started off in Gnosall and then my father branched out into Shropshire. John and I are carrying on the tradition: we honour the tried-and-trusted methods but we are not afraid to innovate."

When Hannah began her business, there was only one way to bake bread. In the 21st century there are myriad versions.

Richard said: "Things have changed a lot during our lifetimes. Don't forget, when my father started, there was no such thing as the sliced loaf. Big commercial bakeries put a lot of small bakers out of business. But we managed to survive. My father developed a small grocery business and worked with other bakeries to keep going.

"We've always been willing to adapt and adjust. We refuse to give in. There's a never-say-die attitude in our family. My two lads, Robert and John, are not workshy. They turn in 80-hour weeks when they're needed.

"They both come up with new ideas. Robert is creating new markets with Bread2Bake, markets and food festivals. John is very aware of new developments and the computerised way of doing things."

Ultimately, however, it's all about the bake. When all is said and done, the quality that unites the Swift family is its love of baking. Richard said: "None of us enjoy the hassle or bureaucracy. We just love to bake."

A sixth generation is being introduced to the business. Robert's two children, Elliott and Mackenzie, have just started to work markets with their grandmother, Margaret, despite their tender age. They love the work and are set to follow in their predecessors' footsteps.

Margaret said: "All of our family have worked hard. Richard and I have devoted our lives to the business and our family. It's a real joy to bring my grandsons into the fold. We take them to the markets and they get a real buzz from it. They thoroughly enjoy interacting with the customers. It's a real privilege to be able to make them a part of our heritage. We are very proud of all of our children and grandchildren."

For more than 150 years the Swift family has been creating a product of quality and distinction by using traditional baking methods.

Richard added: "One of the best times of the week is early on a Sunday morning when we make the specials for a food festival or market. Then we're bakers again, not businessmen. We're doing it for the love of it. We bake the bread, we sell it directly and the customers tell us whether they like it or not."

For a century-and-a-half, customers have been voting with their feet.

ANDREW RICHARDSON

1 Infancy
2 Adolescence
3 End of adolescence
4 Maturity

THE LIFE OF BREAD

YOUR dough begins its life the moment you plunge your hands into your flour-and-water mix. Bread making has a cycle, the same as life. Dough moves from infancy through adolescence to maturity; these are the three distinct stages.

During the first stage, your dough is like a babe in arms.

- **Infancy**: Why do I call it that? The answer is simple: this first stage is when you have to nurture your dough in order to obtain the best possible results. From the moment you begin to weigh your ingredients through to their initial mix, the dough is completely reliant on you. Like a babe in arms, it is unable to do anything for itself.

As a baker, you have to make sure you look after the dough. You have to care for it, ensure that all of the ingredients are accurately weighed and that the dough is correctly hydrated. If you miss a single step, the result will be failure.

When you are making your dough, it is vitally important that you take time and make sure it gets the best start in life. You must make sure you mix it and knead it properly, in order to help it develop.

- The next stage is **adolescence**. This occurs after the dough has been fully proved.

I call this stage adolescence because the dough has bags of 'attitude' – a real 'I'll-do-what-I-like' mood. The well-behaved, infant stage is a thing of the past.

During adolescence, the dough will be sticky and gassy and very hard to handle. When we work with the dough, it almost seems to fight us. It doesn't want to do as it's told; it seems to think it knows best.

As you work the dough, the gluten tightens and it will often rip. The tension in the dough can cause all sorts of problems. Adolescence is the stage when things can unravel – and that is why our moulding section is so important [*see page 30*]. During this stage, you have to control your dough by moulding it to fit in with what you need.

Experience is a great ally and will help you to understand how to shape the dough so that you get the desired result. If we handle our dough correctly during this stage and are firm with it, the final bake will be considerably better.

- The third and final stage in the life of bread is **maturity**. At this point, your bread's life is complete. You will have helped the bread mature into the best loaf that it can possible be. Success or failure hinges on whether or not you have handled the dough properly during its infancy and adolescence. So make sure you look after it during those formative stages. Look after it, give it what it needs, tell it what to do and then sit back and reap your rewards.

2
3
4
1
9
8
7
5
6

Tools of the Trade

HOME bakers don't need to spend a fortune if they want to learn how to make their own bread. Other than a good oven, a decent table or working surface and a few essentials, you should be good to go.

There are a few pieces of kit that you ought to buy. Don't worry, they don't cost the earth and all are sufficiently robust to last for several years.

1 **Metal scraper** – used to clean down surfaces, cut dough and scrape out mixing bowls. They are very versatile. Better-made varieties can also be used for chopping herbs. It can also be used when manipulating dough while mixing.

2 **French blade** (or lame, pronounced 'lahm'), used to score the surface of dough. Lames come with different types of blade, some straight and some curved. Those with a straight blade are held perpendicular to the loaf's surface and are often used for round loaves. Those with curved blades are used for long breads, such as baguettes.

3 **Measuring spoons** – precision is everything to the baker and measuring spoons will save you time and energy. They'll help you get accurate mixes.

4 **Plastic scraper** – just as important as a metal scraper. They'll help you to remove every last bit of dough or cake mix from the interior of a mixing bowl. They're moulded so should fit inside most bowls.

5 **Cake tins** – come in all shapes and sizes these days. Every baker should have 1lb and 2lb tins.

6 **Mixing bowl and sieve** – a good mixing bowl is something that you can't do without. You also need a sieve, so that you can sift flour when it's required to keep your bakes light.

7 **Whisk** – to whip air into sauces, creams and icings.

8 **Spatula** – used in a similar way to a plastic scraper. Its long handle gives you a greater reach.

9 **Wooden spoon** – a great investment. Wooden spoons are simultaneously inexpensive and indispensable. Buy a range of sizes.

Other tools that you might like to invest in include:

- **Spray bottle** for spraying water onto doughs, if you want to stick seeds to them. They are also good for creating steam when you load dough into the oven.
- **Measuring jug** to give you precise results when measuring liquids.
- **Brush** for covering the tops of dough and pastry with oil, butter or egg wash.
- **Rolling pin**. Seek out long and heavy varieties for specialist tasks, like making croissant dough, as well as an all-purpose one for pastry.
- **Scales** (digital). An absolute must, though I also use weighing scales with metal weights. Our family's been using them for 150 years.
- **Proving mould** to prove sourdoughs.
- **Clean, smooth surface**. Not everyone has a big kitchen table!
- **Olive oil** – used as an ingredient and to finish doughs with a good sheen.

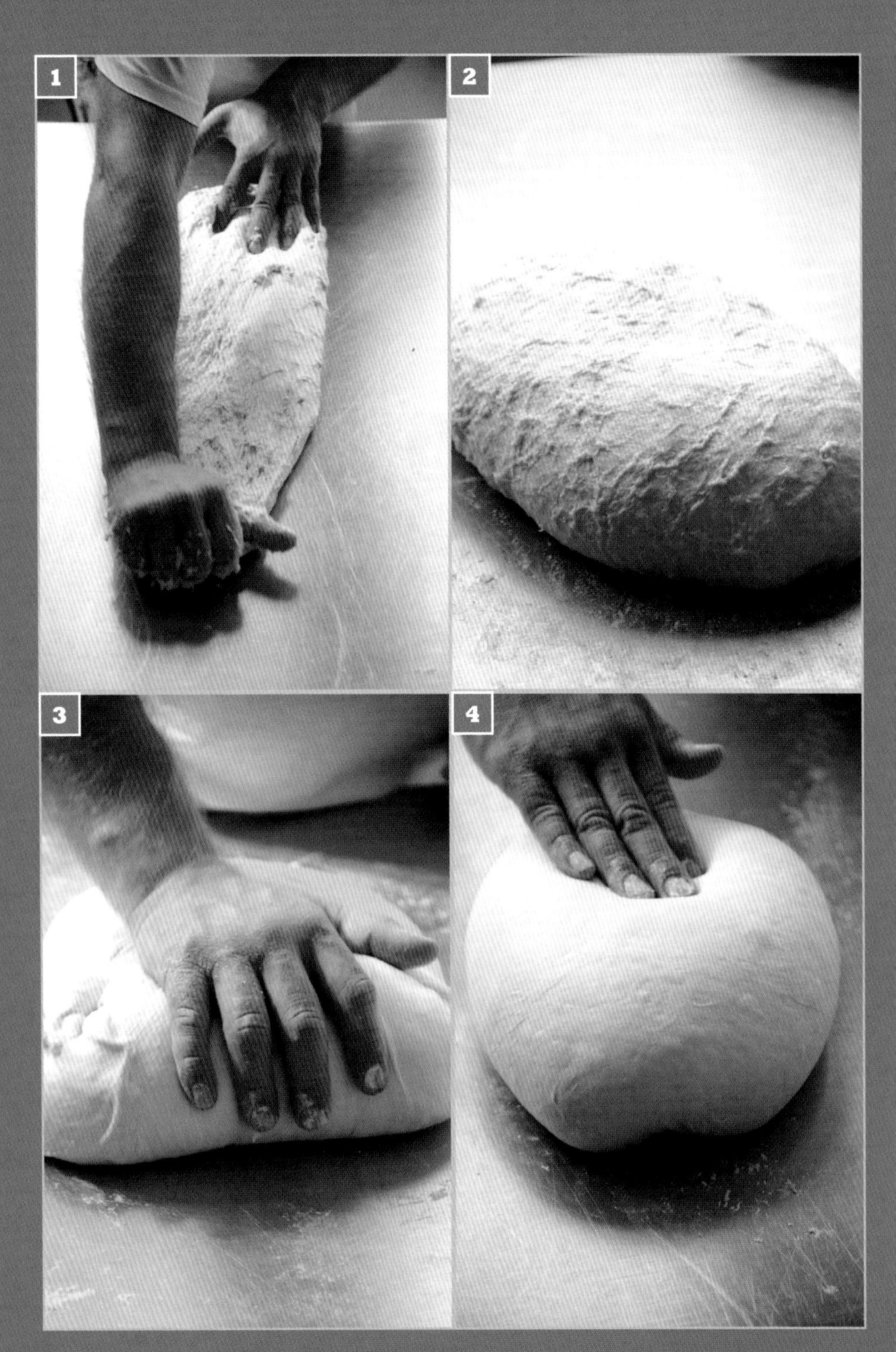
1
2
3
4

Gluten, Resting and Other Essentials

AS soon as water is added to your flour, gluten makes an appearance. Gluten is a protein composite found in foods processed from wheat. It gives elasticity to dough and helps it to rise. It is also responsible for giving bread its chewy texture.

Gluten is found in the protein of your flour and it is an essential component of the breadmaking process. Without gluten, you would not be able to bake a loaf. Gluten is the composite of gliadin and glutenin, which is found in wheat. It was discovered by Buddhist monks during the seventh century during their search for a meat substitute.

I always think of gluten as being similar to electricity. It is present within flour all the time – just as electricity is present in a wall socket. But you have to turn it on, or activate it, for it to become evident – just as you have to flick the switch of your plug.

The gluten benefits from our kneading of the dough. The kneading process helps us to create a gluten framework – and that is the key to a great bake. By producing a good gluten framework, we will produce a good dough. A good dough will yield a good loaf.

So how do we develop a good gluten framework? To find the answer, think about how you would develop a muscle. Muscles need to be exercised and then rested in order for them to develop, just as the gluten framework in our dough develops through kneading. However, the muscle develops when it is at rest. That is when it takes time to repair and absorb the energy it received during exercise. Dough is the same. Giving dough periods of rest allows the gluten to repair itself from the pounding it took when it was being kneaded. That rest period allows the gluten to develop, which improves the quality of our dough.

A good gluten framework leaves our dough feeling soft, smooth and easy to handle. To illustrate the point, think of an elastic band. If you take a elastic band and pull it suddenly, the tension will be too great and it will snap. However, if you take the same elastic band and stretch it a little at a time, you'll find yourself able to stretch if further. Eventually, it will stretch to its full potential without breaking.

By constantly kneading and resting our dough, we are giving it the opportunity to become more elastic. Gradually, the gluten framework will improve.

Standard doughs should be given a

1 Kneading dough, which is rough and rips easily.
2 During the first rest, the dough is coarse.
3 Further kneading strengthens the gluten content.
4 Our final dough has a smooth surface and 'bounce'.

The Gluten Framework

H_2O = Water
Y = Yeast
S = Salt
F/Su = Fat and sugar

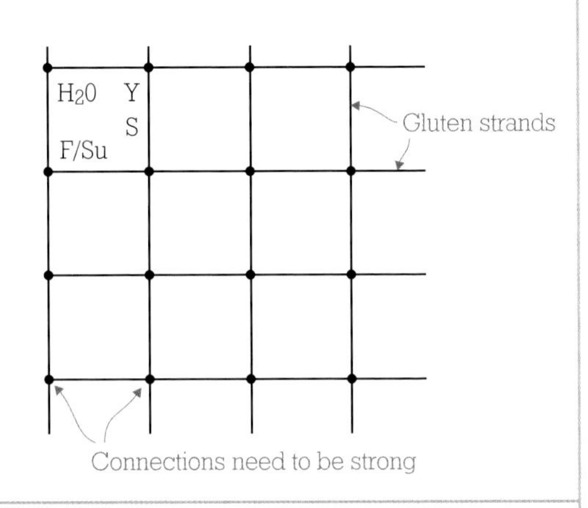

As the yeast works, the framework must change. Gluten strands need to expand as the yeast produces carbon dioxide, sugars, etc.

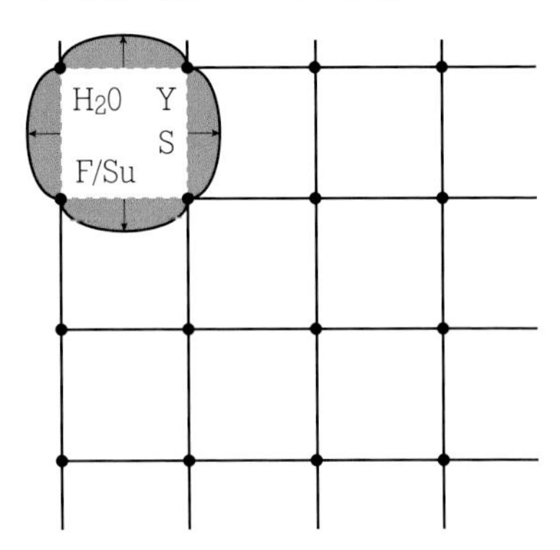

If framework not properly developed, the strands will break and the dough will collapse unaided, either in tin from table to oven, or while in the oven in tin or on tray.

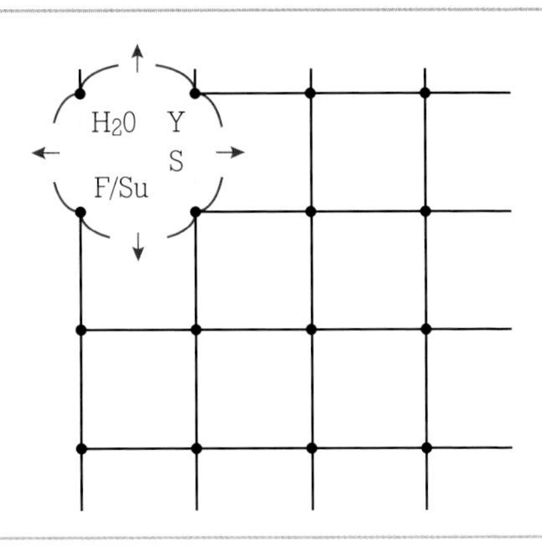

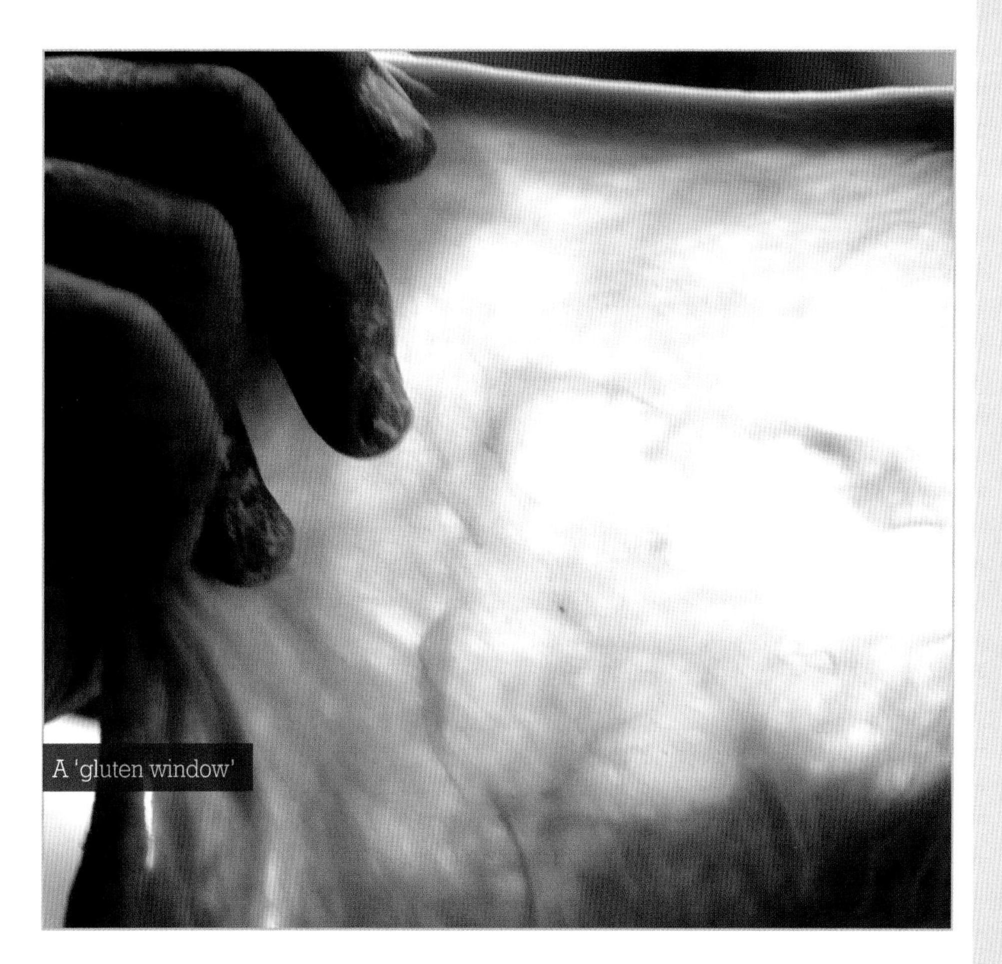
A 'gluten window'

minimum of two rest periods, which should each be between five and six minutes long. Those periods should be interspersed with kneading. There are recipes that require greater kneading and resting and I will highlight those on subsequent pages.

The principles of the gluten framework are illustrated opposite.

To create a good gluten framework, we need good hydration. This will be explained subsequently, when I discuss the water method. A good framework also requires good strength from working and stretching the dough. Finally, it requires periods of resting, which allows the gluten framework to develop. Those factors combine to create a good gluten framework, which you can check by creating a 'gluten window' (above).

The formula is simple:
Kneading + Resting = Good Gluten Framework = Consistent Dough = GOOD BREAD

1 Pouring yeasty water into a flour-and-salt mix.
2 Mixing with your hands helps you determine the wetness of the mix.
3 You can add more water as you go.
4 Your dough should still be sticky when you removc it from the bowl.

Water Method

WATER is crucial to our dough: too much or too little will result in the 'life of our bread' being affected! The key to getting this right is not to add all of your water at once. By doing this it gives you some control over the final dough. But *how*, and *why*?

Firstly, even though you may always use the same type of flour from the same shop, the actual quality of the flour may fluctuate, due to the type of grain used, the age of the grain, where it has come from, etc.

For example, the moisture content of your flour can change depending on the condition of the wheat used. Flour will be tested for moisture content and will be acceptable provided it falls within upper and lower limits – but flour with a higher moisture content won't take the same amount of water. Hence if you always use the same amount, your doughs will automatically be inconsistent. By working your water in *in stages* you can control the water content of your dough.

Another reason for doing this involves our dough/gluten development. In the previous section we used the illustration of a muscle and how working that helped to strengthen it. This same procedure is linked with water too!

As we work the gluten and develop that framework, as well as becoming stronger our gluten becomes more absorbent, thus allowing us to make sure our doughs are properly hydrated. By adding water gradually we can see and feel how the dough is changing. We need to make sure the dough is well hydrated in our bowl before we bring it out onto the table to begin kneading. The dough has to be sticky and wet to allow the gluten to absorb the water as it becomes stronger through kneading.

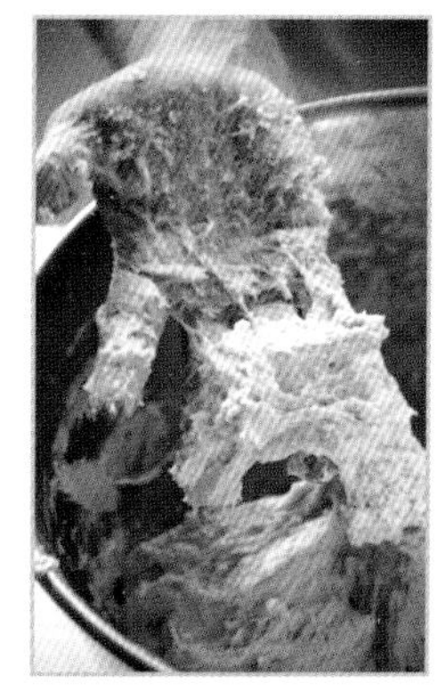

Your dough should be sticky – but not wet.

- Gluten worked becomes stronger.
- As it becomes stronger it becomes more absorbent.
- It starts to take in water and reduce stickiness.
- 'Bounce' becomes softer.
- The gluten framework becomes supple.
- Result: A good dough!

TOP TIP: Always measure 20ml water less than the recipe states. (When writing a recipe I always put a slightly reduced amount in anyway – it helps to make sure all the yeast is worked into the dough. As my dad and granddad would say, it's easier to put in than to take out!

This should be the way to approach any dough you make unless it is stated within the recipe.

1
2
3
4

Basic White Dough

ONCE you've mastered the technique for making a basic white dough, you'll be up and running. A basic white dough is the foundation upon which most recipes are built. There is still more to learn, of course. Other sections deal with flours, moulding and tips for perfect bakes. Individual recipes might also require different resting times, or alternative kneading techniques.

But if you're able to make a basic white dough you're more than halfway to being a baker.

We focused on the importance of the mixing stage earlier; looking at the life of bread and the way it passes from infancy through adolescence to maturity. It is impossible to underplay the importance of good mixing: this is where you shape the future of your loaf.

Let's follow a step-by-step process, so you can learn how to make a basic white dough. The individual quantities required for particular recipes are outlined later in the book. This section helps you to understand how to use those ingredients.

Firstly, weigh your dry ingredients into a bowl. This will include flour and salt. Using your hands, work the salt into the flour. This stage should not be overlooked. When you later add your yeasty water, you do not want it to come into contact with neat salt.

Now weigh your water and add the yeast to it. Always remember the water method when you are doing this.

Add your yeasty water to the flour and slowly begin to work them together, introducing the water to the flour. You will begin to see the effects of the gluten as your dough starts to form. Dry dough and flour will still be present at this stage, so use your extra water to start hydrating that. Work the dough together and watch as it starts to change. Continue to spot in water and combine by using your hands, as highlighted in the water method section [*see page 25*], until all of the flour has disappeared. There should now be a difference in colour between the dough and the initial flour.

Pinch test

At this point, pinch the dough between your thumb and fingers. You must make sure the dough feels the same all the way through. It must have a soft, sticky feel and there should be no dry flour. When pinching, also make sure there are no tight knots – if you have those, the only way to get rid of them is by adding water and working it directly into them.

Once your dough has reached the state

1 Measure your flour and salt into a mixing bowl.
2 Mix thoroughly, using your hands.
3 Work the dough by stretching it away from you.
4 Fold the dough back towards you.

Pinch test

where it is soft, tacky and sticky, you should tip it out onto the table or your work surface. You might feel as though you should add more flour because the dough will be quite sticky. However, resist the temptation!

Now you're ready to begin the kneading/mixing process.

Start to work the dough vigorously and firmly, by stretching it away from you, then folding it back towards you. Continue that action until the dough takes in any residual water and loses its stickiness.

The dough should be starting to firm up and you should feel the difference as the dough becomes easier to handle. Once the dough reaches this point, continue to work it for a further five minutes, then allow it a five-minute rest.

Now take the rested dough and work it firmly with considerable downwards force. You may observe it ripping and stretching – do not be alarmed if it does. As you work the dough, the gluten will tighten and so will the dough. It will start to feel sticky again, but don't panic – keep working it until the dough has a rough finish, like crinkly cabbage. Now rest it for a second time.

Once the dough has rested, pick up the ball and use folding techniques to get it ready for its final prove. Knead the dough and then fold it back on itself, before turning it 90 degrees and repeating that motion. You do not want to take it to the point where it starts to rip. After five minutes, give it a final rest.

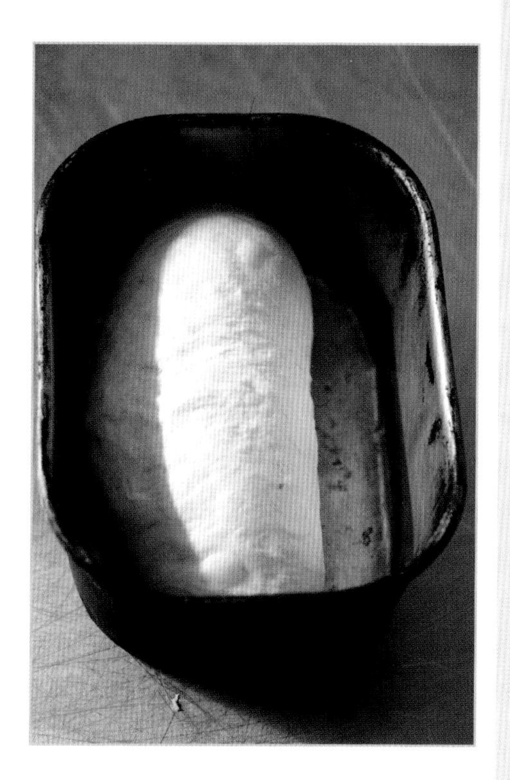

You can run through the following checklist, to be confident that it's complete:

1 None of the four ingredients should be individually visible.
2 The dough should have a smooth finish.
3 The dough should have a buoyancy and resistance to touch.
4 The dough should sit up well on the table and not collapse.
5 Check for a gluten window. To do that, simple pinch a small piece of dough and stretch it until it becomes translucent. The light should peer through it and it should not tear or snap.

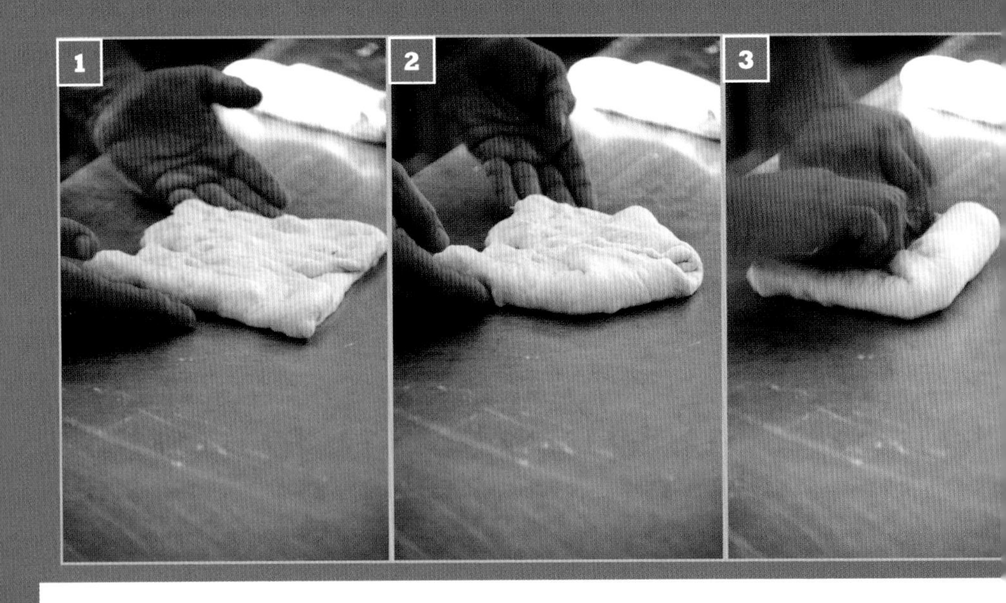

MOULDING TECHNIQUES

WE'VE examined kneading and proving, but you also need to be able to moulding your dough before baking. Here are four basic shapes that will serve you well.

● **Tin loaf.** (See pictures above). When moulding this loaf we need to use our knuckles to push out the dough. Remember our dough is in its adolescent stage and it is relatively easy to tell it what to do. First push it out into a long rectangle horizontally across the table, then bring in both sides to make our oblong into a square (**1**). The seam you create needs to be pushed down so it disappears. Once here fold the top two corners in to create a 'house' effect (**2**). Now take the top of the point of the 'roof' and fold it over, then loosely roll up towards you (**3**). This should result in a swiss-roll effect. Take this and turn it 90 degrees so that it is running vertically up the table.

Turn it over so the crease faces towards the ceiling (**4**). The dough should feel quite tight, so we need to be firm and direct. With your dough on the table, begin to push it out again to give you an oblong running vertically up the table (**5**). Take the two corners at the top – as we did to make our house – then fold over the point of the roof. Begin to roll towards you, but as you roll this time push in with your fingers to give it the tightest mould possible. Place the

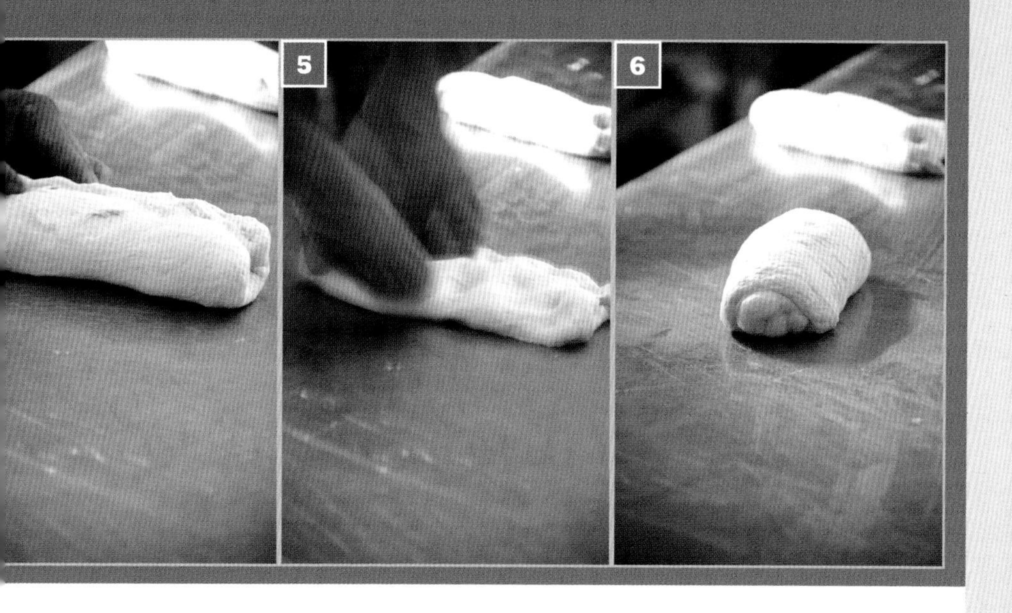

finished loaf (**6**) crease-side down in an oiled tin.

● **Batch loaf**. This loaf starts off life in a very similar way to the tin loaf. We use our knuckles to push out our dough into an oblong shape. However, do not be as vigorous as you were with the tin loaf. Push out into a square then roll up. It should be quite loose as we are about to put our mould onto our bread. Turn the dough 90 degrees so it is vertical up the table, but this time with the crease on the underside. Using the palm of your hand push down on the side of the dough. Now push forward from the tip of our fingers to the heel of your hand. Always push forward in a straight line, although your head may be telling you to go round in a circle. Continue this motion, always bringing your loaf back to the start point on the table. Push forward and bring back, push forward and bring back. You need to put a firm pressure on your dough, probably a little more than you would think. You should end up with a nice round loaf with the underside of your loaf looking similar to a cauliflower. That is the part that you would place onto the baking tray.

1
2
3
4

● **Bloomer**. This loaf is a little different in the fact that we now employ what is called a 'double mould', which helps to firm up the dough and develop the gluten without tearing or ripping. Begin in exactly the same vein as the tin loaf, working out to an oblong, then to a square, and on to a 'house with a roof'. Once we are at this point, rather than just loosely rolling up we mould it tightly. Using your thumbs, push the dough inwards as you roll it towards you. When you have a swiss roll, cover and leave for 10 minutes.

Now take your rested dough and place it, crease-side up, along its length horizontally. Push out just as you did before, following exactly the same pattern: oblong, square, house. When you roll up for a second time again use your thumbs to push in the dough. As your dough rolls up to the point where it is nearly complete, use your hands to push down on either side of the dough as you roll back and forth so you taper the ends to a point.

● **Rolls**: (See pictures opposite). The mould for rolls is very different but once mastered will give great results. There'll be no more flat rolls that collapse in the oven!

To begin with pull your dough out into a rough oblong. Fold your dough over and over along its horizontal line, pushing down as you go. Keep doing that until you have rolled your dough into a sausage shape (**1**). Make sure it is as even as possible, to help produce even-sized rolls. Then mark off equal sections along your dough (**2**), cut through and divide them up using a plastic dough cutter. Place one of the dough pieces in the palm of your hand, then cup your hand. Now place the dough on the table, with your hand still over it (**3**). Then push down gently and make a circular motion. As you feel the dough tighten in your hand, continue to make a circular motion and use the whole of your hand to make the loaf round – so roll it clockwise, using your fingers against the dough at 12 o'clock and your palm at 6 o'clock. The more pressure you can apply the better the rolls will be (**4**). Don't be afraid to push down on the dough, you have to master it. Use a double mould method, by resting them once for five minutes and then repeating the method. That tightens the rolls and allows the gluten to develop. Prove before baking.

SALT

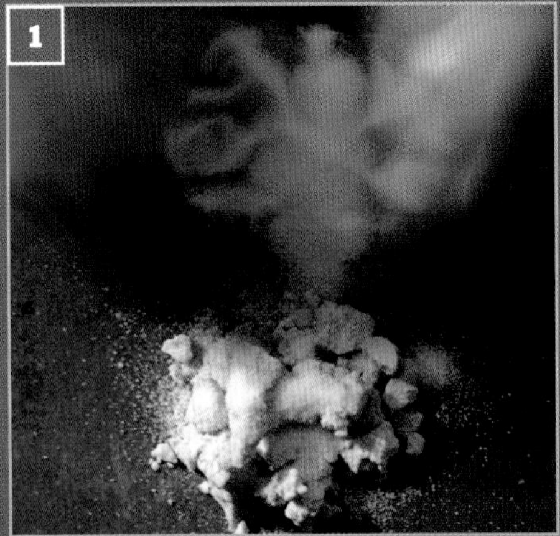

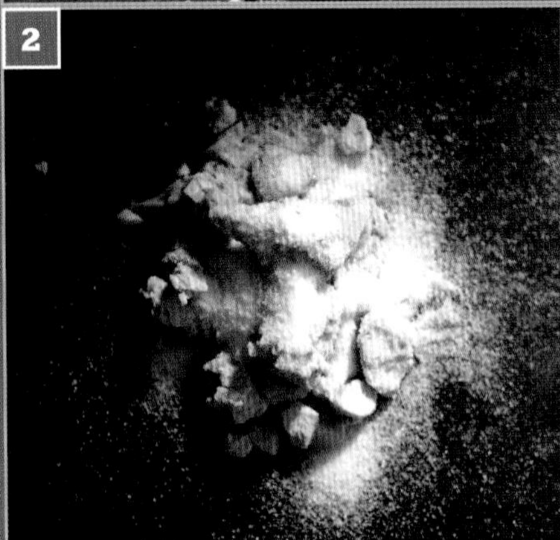

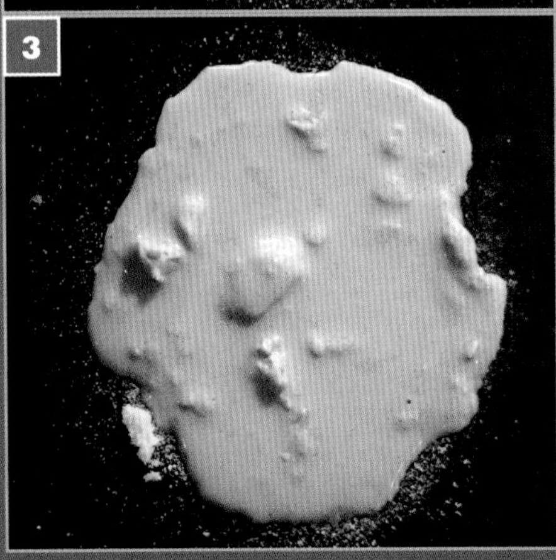

THE use of salt today in foods is a hotly debated topic. The debate rages just as fiercely when it comes to baking bread.

In the relationship between bread and salt, there is one immutable fact: bread needs salt. Bread without salt simply doesn't work: it is horrible and bland, irrespective of what other flavourings you might use. Salt draws out the natural flavours and enhances them. There is, however, much more to the bread-salt relationship than flavour.

Salt works in at least five stages of our dough production.

- It helps to enhance the taste and flavour of your loaf.
- It helps to control and balance the fermentation process.
- It helps to firm-up the gluten framework.
- It helps to retain moisture in the dough.
- It works as a natural preservative by inhibiting certain types of mould growth.

The regulation of taste is fairly straightforward, so I'll move on swiftly to the way that salt controls and balances the fermentation process. To understand how that works, we have to look at the relationship between salt and yeast.

1 Salt is added to yeast.
2 The two react.
3 The yeast is destroyed – the 'slug effect'.

Put simply, the two just don't get on. When salt comes into direct contact with yeast, it spells curtains for the yeast. We call this the 'slug effect': putting salt on yeast is like putting salt on a slug. It's not pretty.

But if salt and yeast have a mutual antipathy, why do we put both into our dough? Surely it can only lead to problems.

Actually, the use of salt in dough is entirely necessary. Once salt and yeast are absorbed into the dough – which is easily done using the water method – the salt has a completely different effect: rather than destroying the yeast, it actually acts as a controlling agent. The salt restrains the yeast and prevents it from producing the gases and sugars too fast. This can ruin the dough. It salt ensures our dough isn't a hit-and-miss affair.

The presence of salt gives us a balanced and even proof, which will give us a nice even-coloured bake. If we don't use salt, we could end up with rather a patchy crust. There will be dark areas where sugars gathered in too high a concentration. The slower and more controlled our fermentation the better it will be for the flavour and colour of loaf. It will also ensure a better taste and make the loaf easier to digest.

Salt also helps to strengthen the gluten framework. As discussed in other areas of the book, our gluten framework is crucial to the production of our dough and ultimately our loaf. Just as lemon juice helps to firm up whipped cream, so salt has a firming effect on gluten, helping to make a strong bond and secure framework.

Salt also helps to keep moisture in our dough. Water content is crucial, and salt can greatly aid the process. If you need an example of how that works, just think about what happens when you put salt in a damp atmosphere. The salt becomes lumpy and aggregates as it draws in moisture. Holding that moisture in will slow down the rate at which the finished bread goes stale. Large bakeries that make mass-produced loaves try to find chemical ways of achieving a similar effect – which results in a loaf that is as fresh on the seventh day as it was on the first. You don't need to be an expert to work out that that is wrong; just think about what you might be eating.

Finally, salt helps to inhibit mould growth. It is a natural preservative and having salt in our dough is enormously helpful. Our bread will go stale before going mouldy, because of the presence of salt.

Salt strenthens the gluten framework

SUGAR

THE use of sugar in bread causes almost as much debate as the use of salt in bread. The principle question is simple: Should we use sugar or not? And if the answer to that is yes, then when should it be used?; in what quantities?; should it be mixed with yeast?; and what purpose does it serve?

I am frequently asked those questions about sugar. The answers are not straightforward.

Sugar is frequently included in recipes containing dry or fast-acting yeast. The reason is simple: sugar works as a 'yeast food', helping to activate and feed the yeast. Very often, the use of sugar is linked to time issues. For example, sugar is likely to be used at schools in home economics classes, where time is of the essence because it helps to cut down proving time.

In this book, I am highlighting the use of fresh yeast or sourdough cultures, so the use of sugar is not as prevalent, because these yeasts they do not require the same levels of feeding. However, that doesn't mean that sugar isn't, or can't be, used.

There are indeed reasons why types of sugar might be used. First, they help to create a soft fermented dough with a quick bake time, which maximises softness. Good examples are soft white or wholemeal baps.

Sugar also affects the colour of the dough because it promotes caramelisation. The more sugar in the dough, the quicker the crust will develop. So, if we 'bake to colour' – that is, by

watching when our bread starts to go brown – our baps will have been baked for a shorter time, which means they will be lovely and light and soft.

Then there is the flavouring of our doughs. For instance, we might want to make sweet fermented doughs or doughs with honey or syrup in them. This area is fraught with problems, however, and I'll explain why. Sugar is a yeast food and like all foods, too much can be a bad thing. If you add an abundant quantity of sugar to your yeast at the wrong time, it will make it dormant. This is particularly true of concentrated liquid sugars such as honey, treacle or syrup. Adding those at the wrong time can have disastrous effects on dough.

That happens because the sugars smother the yeast, crystallising around it and stopping it from working. It is too much for the yeast to handle and results in a dead, unactive dough, which feels like used chewing gum.

Where sugars are used in sizeable recipes in this book, I will highlight the point at which they should be used. As a rule of thumb, however, if we want to add a honey or a similar substance, we should always do that when the dough is beginning to form together in the mixing bowl, just as the flour is beginning to disappear. The dough helps to protect the yeast from the sugars being added.

As regards sweet fermented doughs, the quantity of sugar can be quite high. So to combat that we can mix a ferment which is similar to the process that people will remember from school home economics. That consists of water, sugar, milk powder, and flour to thicken: a fuller explanation will be given in the section for 'sweet breads and cakes'.

In short, our objective when baking is to give the yeast a good start in life so that it can ferment. It is best to do that before we add the rest of the sugar and create the dough.

Oils and Fats

WHEN you have mastered your basic dough-making to a point where you are getting consistent results you will probably want to start ringing a few changes and trying different things. One easy way of doing that is to add oil to your dough. This shouldn't be mistaken for adding fat: the purpose of using oil is mainly to flavour and soften your dough, giving you a different overall texture and finished loaf.

The question then arises: What oil should you use? Well, olive oil is always good, especially if it's extra virgin. There are plenty out there. I favour oils that are thick and deep in colour. I also favour some Sicilian oils, which have nice grassy notes. You don't have to stop at olive oil, however. You might like to try something a little different, maybe rapeseed oil, which lends itself nicely to carrying other flavours. Rapeseed is particularly pleasant when its been smoked. It works both *in* and *on* your bread.

There is one important point relating to the addition of oils to your dough: *never* use them as a water replacement. Although your oil often softens the dough, it does not hydrate the gluten in the same way as water. That means you could be affecting your gluten framework and ultimately your dough. You'll also find your final loaf short of water. The oil won't be able to keep the bread moist when you bake it. If you have ever made olive-oil biscuits, you will know they have quite a snap to them as they are poorly hydrated. I suggest you add the oil at a similar point at which you would add honey: so, once the dough has begun to pull together and take in the flour, add your oil and begin to mix it in. Once the oil goes back into your dough, go back to adding your water (as explained in the section on 'water method'). Make sure you gain the same consistency as you would in a dough without oil.

It's time to consider the use of fat in our breadmaking. Fat, like sugar, can feed yeast, though it isn't as effective as sugar. Fat is more frequently used when working with wholemeal flours. The addition of fat to those types of flours helps to break down the bran/fibre content of the flour, which in turn improves the overall condition of the dough.

Other instances where fat can be beneficial is when we are looking to soften the dough – for instance with soft rolls or sweet fermented goods. When there is a need for fat in subsequent recipes, I'll highlight it. In summary, fat is infrequently used in dough.

The addition of other ingredients, such as dried fruit, nuts and seeds can also affect your dough. It can drastically change the texture and flavour of your loaf. One key consideration – as with sugar and fat – is when you should add them.

Malt or hard grains should be added to your dough at the beginning. For example, if you are using malted wheat grains, sunflower seeds, sesame seeds or poppy seeds, you should do so when you are weighing your ingredients and they are still dry. If you were wanting to add a dried herb, or a dry flavouring or spice, this would be at the point where the dough has begun to form in the bowl – though before we've completed the water method. This will enable us to distribute the ingredient through the whole dough as we work it on the table. Dry herbs and powders will, of course, adjust the dryness of our dough, so adding water gradually after that will mean our dough isn't compromised.

The addition of fresh herbs or wet products – for example pastes or olives – should be done after the dough is properly formed. I'll talk you through specific methods on relevant recipe pages.

1 Adding yeast to water. **2** Adding flour to water and yeast. **3** Stirring. **4** Achieving the correct consistency.

POOLISH

POOLISH is a dough preparation made up of yeast, which is combined with 50 per cent water and 50 per cent flour. It does not contain salt. Poolish means 'Polish' in French. Poolish is traditionally left overnight, but you can get away with leaving it for just a few hours. It is a starter made from the same ingredients as the dough and imparts a unique flavour. It also improves the development of the dough.

Poolish has a soft, creamy appearance and the fermentation time will depend on the quantity of yeast. As it is a starter, the quantity used in the final dough can be anything from a third, to a half, even three quarters of the overall volume.

There are reasons for choosing this method. Using poolish helps with the development of the dough's gluten framework. It also helps the overall development of the dough. It can reduce the kneading time required and also lends itself to the creation of a smoother dough. And having a smooth dough is key to a great bake.

Poolish will also give your crumb a honeycomb effect and it gives your bread a tangier taste. Poolish is not as strong as sourdough, but it is certainly different from a 'straight' dough. The final bread also has a longer chew, which allows you to fully taste the flavour of your bread. The bread will also last a little longer than a regular bread, not going stale quite so quickly.

The technique is often used in the production of French and Italian breads. The Italian equivalent is a 'biga'.

The organoleptic characteristics of poolish are a light hazelnut aroma, standard volume, yellow and open crust, and weak acidity.

Making poolish is simple. Place your water in the mixing bowl and add yeast. Mix it until it dissolves. Then add flour to the liquid and mix well until all of the flour and water are mixed together. This creates a 'liquid dough', which has a thick, soup-like consistency.

You can leave your poolish in the fridge or at room temperature, depending on how long you want it to ferment. Always keep poolish covered – you don't want to return to your kitchen to find it's leapt out of the mixing bowl!

FLOURS AND INGREDIENTS

WITHOUT flour we would have nothing: no bread, no pastry, no sweet dough. A lot of the food we eat and enjoy today just wouldn't exist.

Flour really is a truly remarkable ingredient. Just consider, for a moment, its mysterious ability to interact with water, heat, and yeast, be it baker's yeast or natural leavening organisms, to create our finished loaf. Flour not only reacts with airborne organisms but also helps the fermentation of sourdough products, as it contains natural organisms. Flour is used to start that process and also aids its progression.

Wheat is split into two categories: hard grain and soft grain. The harder grains are often grown in the US and Canada where the soil is able to cope with the demands of robust wheats; softer grains are more commonly grown in Europe where the soil is less hardy. However, that isn't a hard-and-fast rule, particularly as farming and milling techniques evolve. Wheat can change from harvest to harvest and mills have to be aware of seasonal and regional variations in quality. Each batch of flour will be slightly different from the one before, and bakers need to be receptive to such fluctuations.

The questions I am most often asked on my baking courses concern which types of flour should be used. The answer, however, is not straightforward because the types of flours available these days are so varied. It can be a little confusing.

The first thing to remember is that if you are starting to bake bread for the first

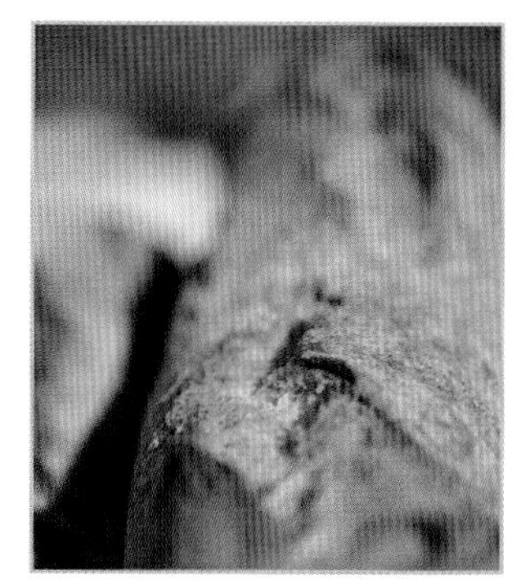
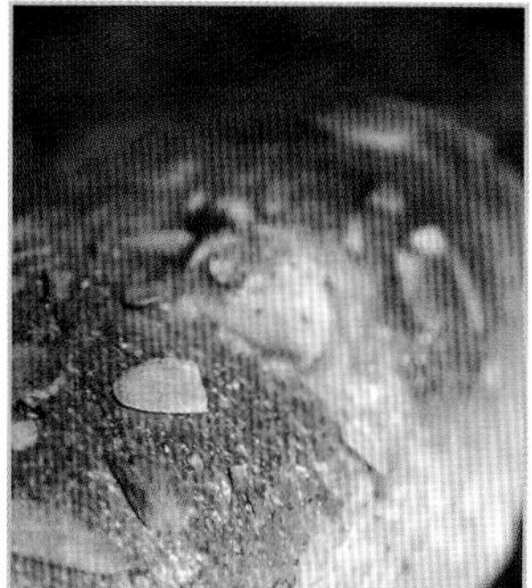

time, or you are wanting to hone your skills, it is always good to use a flour that is going to help you. You need a flour that is going to hold your hand a little and work with you, not against you.

Flour is made up of two parts: starch and protein. Starch is a food source for yeast; it is converted into sugars during fermentation and proving [*see page 36*]. Protein gives us gluten, which is formed when the water is added to the flour [*see page 21*].

As a baker, you are looking for a flour with quite a high protein content, ideally around 12.0–12.5 per cent. There are flours that have a protein content of 13.5–14.0 per cent. Those are readily available. However, such high gluten flours are best used for speciality breads such as Normandy rye and bagels, where the objective is to obtain a nice chewy, dense texture.

There are additional levels of detail. Two flours can have the same protein content but yield a different quality of gluten. Quality is the determining factor when you are seeking a great bake and this is why the water method is so important – it helps us to adjust our mixing based on how the flour is reacting. For the most part, the stronger the gluten the longer it will need to be mixed, the more water it will absorb, and the longer we can ferment it.

We will be using a variety of flours in the *Born & Bread* recipes, including white, wholemeal, spelt, rye, durum and blends of those. We will also we will be using different French and Italian flours. A lot of the flours we will use are available to buy in supermarkets or specialist retailers, but I will try to give an alternative if possible.

On a personal note, I love working with French wheats, which are usually graded T45/55/65 for white flours and T130/150/170 for levels of rye flour. The white flours are especially versatile and make good soft doughs but with great elasticity and usability. They are also great to use for speciality loaves, when you are trying to do something a little different.

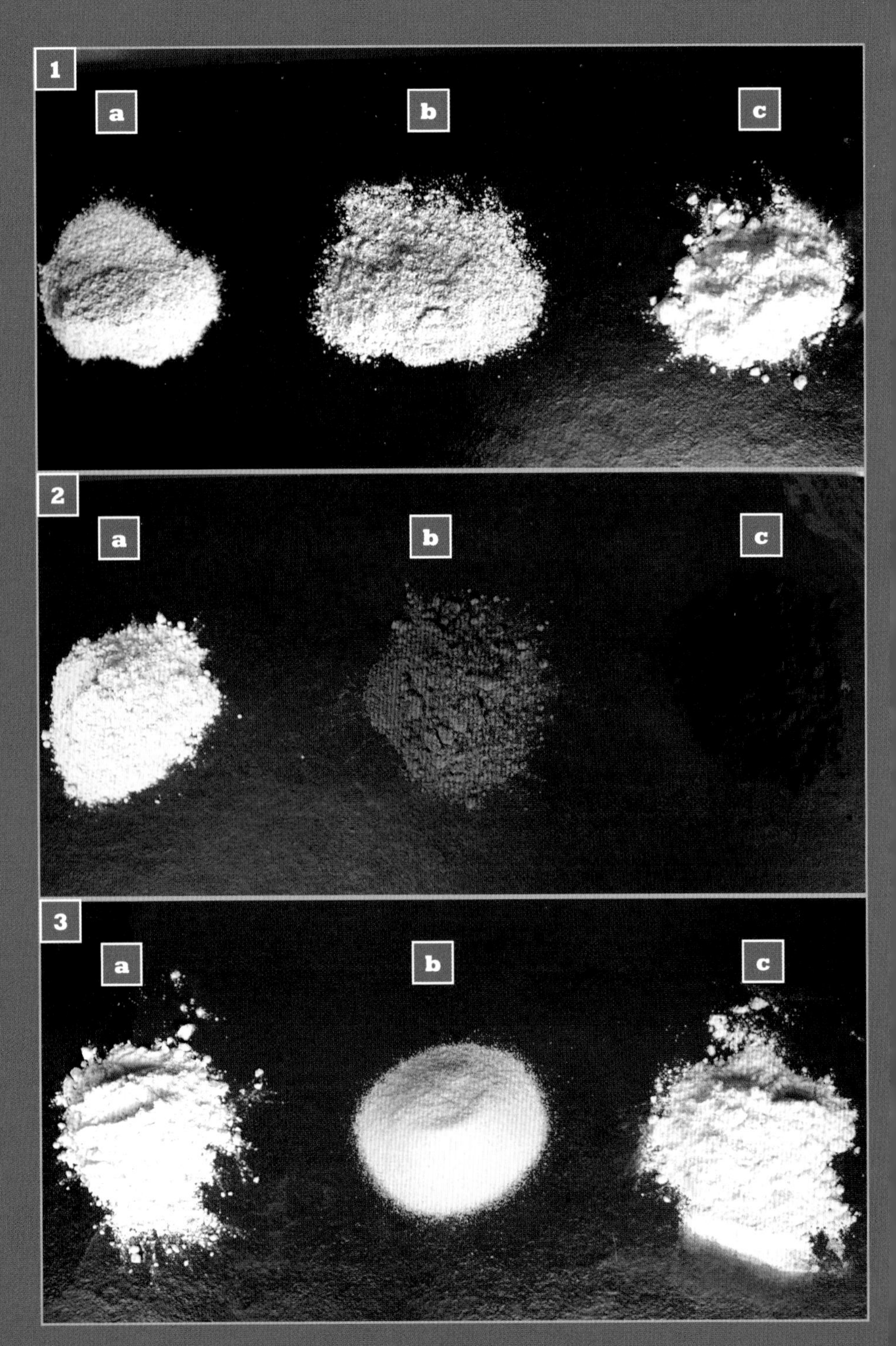
1
a
b
c
2
a
b
c
3
a
b
c

SLATE 1

(**a**) **Basic white flour**. Strong white bread flour is usually a blend of grains from England, Canada and eastern Europe. For breadmaking you want to be looking for a strong bread flour with a protein content of 12.5 per cent or higher. Protein contents can go up to about 15 per cent – however, they may not necessarily be suitable for a traditional white loaf. Gluten is created by protein content: the basic rule of thumb is that a higher protein content gives a higher gluten content. In turn, that provides a better dough to work with, which leads to a better loaf.

(**b**) **Wholemeal**. I use Bacheldre Mill wholemeal flour. I favour their stoneground wholemeal, which gives a very distinctive flavour. As the stone grinds the kernels they get a little bent, which creates a unique flavour. The flour contains the whole grain, including the bran and the fibre, which alters the mixing process. There has been a mill at Bacheldre since 1575 and the current building was created in 1747. That puts our family's 150-year baking heritage into context!

(**c**) **Rye**. Go for 100% rye, which is naturally low in gluten. This flour is particularly useful for those who struggle to eat wheat. It's a wheat-free flour but it shouldn't be mistaken for gluten-free. It usually makes for a very dense, heavy loaf and is also ideal for sourdough starters.

SLATE 2

(**a**) **Diastatic malt flour** is a little similar to Horlicks and is ideal for creating a salty dough. The flour – diastatic enzyme active malt flour, to give it its correct name – is made from finely ground malted barley. It gives an improved rise, softer crumb and more crust colour development without the need for adding sugar. Expect it to add a stickiness and a tackiness to your dough.

(**b**) **Extratone** will add a light malty flavour to your dough. It is a non-diastatic dark malt flour (maltone is another), which is milled from barley malt and has been roasted to a medium golden-brown colour with a high natural malt flavour. It has a wide range of applications in bread and provides good flavour and colour. It is useful in malted granary-type breads and adds a little sweetness to the final dough. It has a pronounced flavour and is used in the production of continental dark breads.

(**c**) **Dark chocolate malt** is a non-diastatic flour that has a very strong, almost bitter flavour. It is specifically used to give a deep, dark, almost-black colour to the final loaf. It has a cigar-like, smokey, tobacco flavour and packs a powerful punch. It is perfect for adding flavour and colour that is reminiscent of both dark chocolate and burnt coffee.

(We use all three in our Shropshire brown loaf; the last one adds the flavour.)

SLATE 3

(**a**) **French T65 flour** – this is a nice, creamy flour. It is as close to traditional plain flour as you'll get. It is great for making traditional French baguettes.

(**b**) **Durum semolina**. Durum refers to wheat and semolina means semi-milled, or half-milled. Durum semolina is a very course milled flour. When added to doughs it breaks down the crumb a little

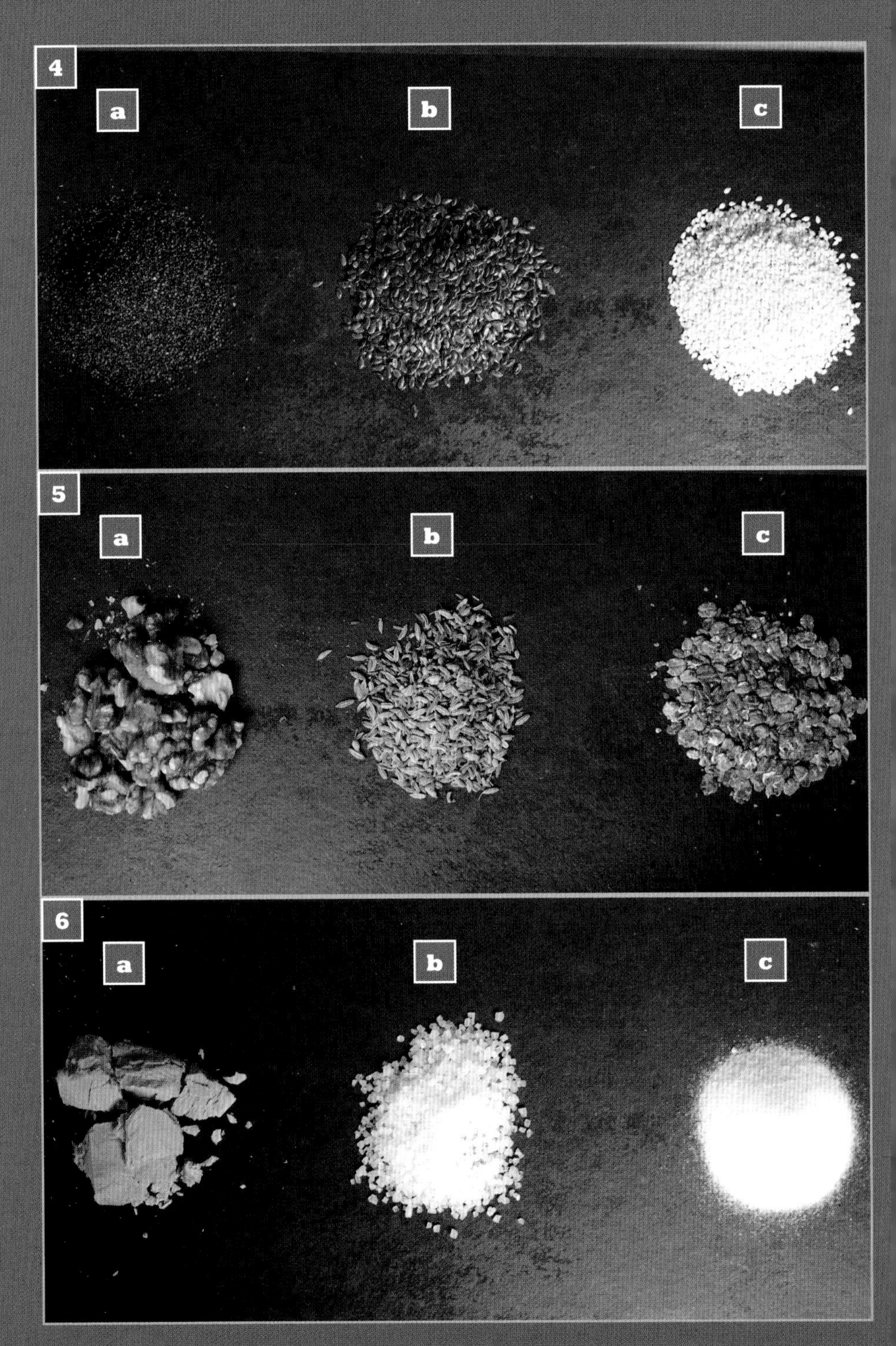
4
a
b
c
5
a
b
c
6
a
b
c

bit and gives you a melt-in-the-mouth fizz. It is ideal for focaccia and Stromboli. It provides a lovely crust and a melt-in-the-mouth centre.
(**c**) **Italian '00' flour**. This is perfect for pasta-making. It is very fine and is also ideal for focaccia and Stromboli. It will absorb a good quantity of water and hold that in the dough to give you a nice, soft mix.

SLATE 4

(**a**) **Poppy seed**. These are oilseeds obtained from the opium poppy. They are harvested from dried seed pods and can be used whole or ground. They add great flavour to breads and can be used inside or on top. They add a distinctive finish and texture to your bake.
(**b**) **Linseed**. This is also known as flax and is grown in cooler climates. Linseed is a good source of omega-3 oils. The seeds have been eaten around the world since ancient times. They come in a range of different colours and preparations, from brown to golden.
(**c**) **Sesame seeds**. These grow in pods and are considered to be the oldest oilseed crop known to man, with a 3,000-year history. Sesame plants are very tolerant to drought and tend to survive when other crops fail. The world harvest amounts to almost 4 million metric tonnes of sesame seeds each year. Toast them before you put them into bread, to activate the oils and enhance their flavour.

SLATE 5

(**a**) **Walnuts**. These work well with any type of pesto-sauce-based breads, but also with cranberry or other sharp fruits. Walnuts are robust in flavour and the contrast with slightly sour fruit is a treat.
(**b**) **Fennel seeds**. These give a nice aniseed flavour, which works particularly well as the accompaniment to citrus additions to dough, such as lemon juice and zest, or lime. Fennel seeds are highly aromatic and flavourful. Fennel seeds can be used in sweet desserts.
(**c**) **Malted wheat flake**. This is ideal for working into multi-grain breads, particularly those that are of a granary type. We use it in our Shropshire Crunch and it gives a nice malty flavour to the bread. It is equally good used on the outside of the loaf because the flakes toast when the loaf is baked.

SLATE 6

(**a**) **Fresh yeast**. This is a living organism. It feeds and gives your dough good stability, consistency and sustainability. When you make a loaf of bread, you are creating a living thing. The yeast helps you to create that life.
(**b**) **Sea salt**. Years ago, it was said that sea salt was much better for your health. It certainly adds a nice flavour and has a slightly subtler taste than table salt. It also adds a little bit of texture. If you use sea salt, then every now and then you will get a little bit that hasn't worked into the dough, which gives you a distinctive crunch and tang. It is also great for topping breads and gives a nice crunch to the loaf. It can be used to add a good flavour to your loaf.
(**c**) **Table salt**. This is essential to the breadmaker. [*See page 34.*]

Hints and Tips

THERE will be times when you're half way through a recipe and a question will pop into your head. What do I do now? Is it supposed to be like that? I've seen this tip on TV – does it work?

This hints-and-tips section is designed to answer many of those questions and give you the confidence to get the best out of your bake.

DON'T PANIC!

Why have I included this in the hints-and-tips section? Well, to be honest, worrying and panicking when it comes to breadmaking will never, *ever* help. You don't need to be scared of dough or petrified of yeast. You don't need to tremble at the thought of making sourdough or poolish, and you don't need to run to the hills if your dough looks too runny. What should you do? Simple: just retrace your steps. Follow the basic methods we have included in *Born & Bread*: the mixing method, the water method and explanations about why we are doing things in a certain way.

WATER TORTURE

Dough too wet? If you use the water method as set out in the book this shouldn't ever be a major problem, but if it does happen what should you do? Well, I class dough that is too wet as looking like porridge with runs and lumps. If you've not reached that stage, you'll be able to bring it back. Just work in little bits of flour, a little at a time, until you pass the pinch test. Take a deep breath, relax and think about what you need to do. Then carry on. Have faith in yourself and if it's beyond repair, comfort yourself with the fact that we all make mistakes: it's often the quickest way to learn.

In recipes, use the initial quantity of water to make your yeast solution. Then add in extra, in line with the water method. Make sure you follow the tests included in the water method.

THE BOTTOM LINE

Tapping the bottom of your loaf is still the best way to tell whether it is baked or not. Engineers have modified the process, creating fancy thermometers that will tell you the temperature inside your bread, but in my opinion they're a waste of money. When you bake, look for good colour all the way around your loaf, including on the bottom. If it's not coloured, it's probably not cooked. The next test is to tap the bottom of the loaf with your knuckles. Tap it right in the middle and listen out for a hollow sound. That will indicate whether the loaf is cooked all the way through, as bread bakes from the outside in, and the centre is the last part to bake.

FULL STEAM AHEAD

Being able to put steam into the oven will benefit the bake, but how is it done? First, forget putting a tray of water or ice cubes into your oven. Yes, they'll create steam, but they'll also cool the oven and spoil your bake. Steam is only useful for the first 10 minutes of your bake. The moisture on the dough helps it make its final jump, giving a nice even rise. Once the bread has climbed beyond the tin, there's no point adding more steam. Remember, the bread will be releasing water of its own into the oven as it bakes.

The best way to add steam is by squirting it through a simple spray bottle. After placing your bread in the centre of the oven, spray around the oven with the bottle for eight to 10 seconds. *Do not spray directly onto the bread*: that will cause the bread to crimp as the water boils on the top of the loaf. Once you've sprayed, close the door and leave it.

Steam also helps with crust development and the overall appearance of the loaf. However, crust formation is also dependent on getting the steam *out* of the oven. The best way of doing that is by simply opening the oven door about five or ten minutes before your bake is finished (just make sure you stand well back). Release the steam by leaving the door open for five seconds, then close and continue the bake. Don't open the door too early: that causes your loaf to sink.

CUTTING COMMENTS

Cutting the top of your loaf makes loaves look aesthetically pleasing by showing the rip and open texture of the crumb. Cutting bread helps to release the tension of the bread and allows the loaf to jump and rip nicely in the oven. If we don't cut the dough, the steam within will force its way out another way, giving you a misshapen loaf or one that falls to one side or the other.

FOLDS AND TURNS

The phrase 'knocking back' is one used repeatedly in baking books. But what does that mean? One of the questions I am most frequently asked is how to knock back a loaf. First, let me tell you what not to do: don't beat the living daylights out of your dough. At that stage in its life, all it requires is a little gentle correction as it heads from infancy into adolescence. Our aim at this point is to help the dough, not beat it into submission.

In the courses that I run, we refer to the process as making 'folds and turns', rather than 'knocking back'. The aim is to be forceful but not destructive. We put turns and folds on the dough during its bulk fermentation in the bowl. Often this will be just once, but there are some doughs that will require two – or even three – turns and folds.

Turns and folds are carried out when the dough has had its initial proof of between one and two hours. Tip your dough out onto the table (there's no need to flour it), take the sides of your dough and fold into the middle. Now push down with your fingertips. You should see gas bubbles form. You'll also hear them start to pop – it feels as though the dough is talking to you, telling you everything is okay. Now work your way down the dough, from top to bottom, just folding it in a little at a time. Once at the bottom of the dough, pick it up and turn it through 90 degrees. Then continue the process: fold in from the sides, turn 90 degrees, fold in from the

sides and repeat. Always fold towards the centre of your dough. As you do so, the pop of bubbles will start to decrease and the dough will become tighter again: that is good, it's exactly what you want. The process should take between 30 seconds and a minute. You need to make sure your dough has tightened up and has reduced to around the size it was when you finished mixing. At that point return your dough to the bowl, cover and give it its second prove.

The point of turning and folding is so freshen up the dough and allow the yeast to find fresh food and continue its development. It is a vital stage in the process. It clears out the old gases created by fermentation, helping you to create a fabulous loaf.

AT THE DOUBLE

As highlighted in the section on moulding techniques [*see page 30*], putting a double mould on our breads – especially those that are baked on a tray, rather than in a tin – gives much better results. It helps to work and relax the bread before it is worked for a final time, which contributes to a sound and well-developed gluten framework.

COLD COMFORT

Good fermentation is crucial to dough. It helps us to produce the best loaf we can with a good structure and good flavour. Of course, many people might not have enough time in the day to mix, prove and bake. Putting your dough in the fridge to prove overnight is often the answer. Sourdoughs lend themselves very well to this, as do doughs made with a poolish, or the poolish itself.

If we want to rest a straight dough overnight the main concern would be to use the correct amount of yeast. I would suggest halving the yeast content. So, for instance, our basic 500g recipe, which calls for 5g yeast, would now require just over 2g. It is also sensible to make sure the temperature of your water is cool, so that the yeast doesn't get too excited and work too fast. The mixing process is exactly the same and nothing else about the production needs to differ.

The best way of using the fridge is as follows. Make your dough and then complete all of the tests, to make sure it's sound. Now cover it and leave it at room temperature for one hour, to ensure the

Scale
SALTER
00:50

start of fermentation. Then place the dough, still covered in the bowl, into the fridge to prove overnight: 10 to 12 hours will be fine. Afterwards, take your dough out and leave it at room temperature for around an hour so that it loses its chill. Now divide and mould as normal and leave covered to prove. That may take a little longer than an hour, if the chill is still in the dough. Once it's ready, bake as normal and enjoy.

SLOWLY DOES IT

Please, please, please don't try to rush your dough. Give it the time it needs to develop properly. Don't be tempted to use 'fast action' packet yeasts. If you can't get hold of fresh yeast just use normal dried yeast.

FEELING THE HEAT

This is a factor that can make a major difference to your dough. The temperature of the water, of your mixing bowl, of the flour you are using, of your kitchen and even the temperature outside – all will be an influence in your dough production.

So what do you do? Well, the temperature of your water is a key factor because that's the one that you can most easily control. It is a myth that your water needs to be warm, tepid or at blood temperature: bread can be made using cold water. Dough made with cold water may require more mixing, but the end result is still the same.

During the summer months we use cold water when we're making dough for our courses. Though seasonal temperature plays a major part, I want to keep this simple. Cold water straight out of the tap can vary between 15C and 18C. During the hot weather, when summer temperatures hit 25C or more, you should use cold water unless the recipe states otherwise.

As temperatures fall outside they can affect inside temperatures as well. In the colder months you can raise your temperatures to between 30C and 34C, roughly the temperature of half hot, half cold water mixed. This rule can be used if your kitchen is particularly hot or cold.

The objective is to dissolve your yeast. If your water is too hot, you will kill it.

IN THE MIX

In this book we have demonstrated hand-mixing techniques. However, you can use a mixer. When using a mixer, the same rules apply as with hand mixing: we need the same consistency of dough, we use the water method, we begin to mix on a slow speed and then when the flour has been incorporated we increase the speed and add a little more water if necessary. Once the dough has formed it will usually start to wrap itself around the dough hook. If that happens, it's not really mixing it's just spinning around. The best thing to do is stop it, pull it off the hook and rest the dough for four or five minutes.

Do the usual tests when the dough is formed. If it needs more work and rests do this on the table, but the machine will take a lot of the work out of it.

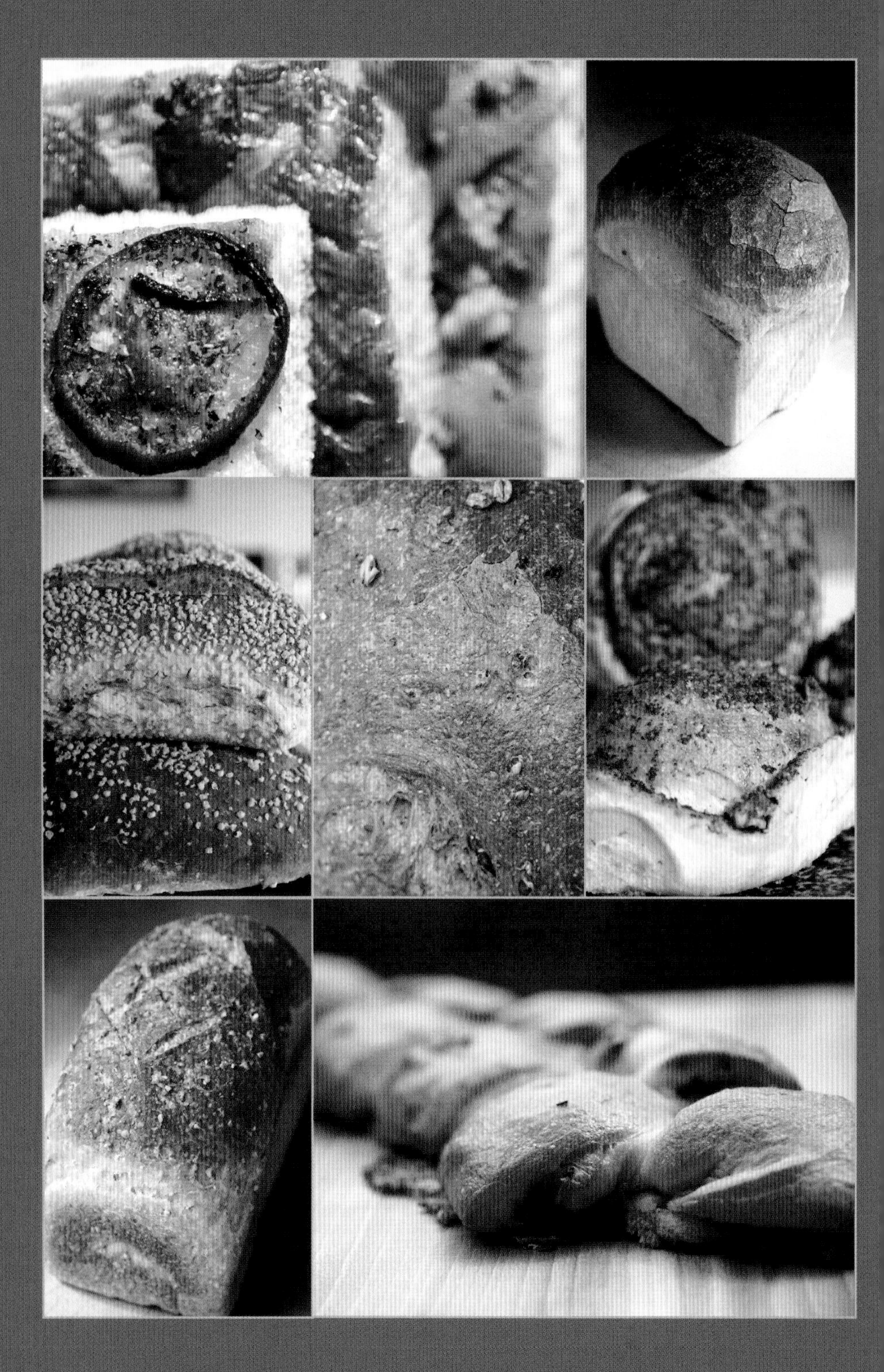

SAVOURY BREADS

Basic White Loaf

THIS is the cornerstone of all bread baking. A basic white loaf was the first loaf that I ever baked – and I've made millions since. Once you've mastered this, you'll be on your way and can look forward to successfully tackling more complex bakes, like sourdough or speciality loaves. Before you begin to bake, refer back to pages 26–29, where we discuss making a basic white dough. You should also refer back to pages 24–25, where we discuss the water method. Finally, you'll need to decide what shape you're looking for: tin, bloomer or rolls. Refer back to pages 30–33 for my tips on moulding techniques before you start.

INGREDIENTS

500g flour
320ml water
8g salt
5g fresh yeast
Extra water, up to 40ml, in accordance with the water method

Makes one 2lb loaf, or two 1lb loaves.

METHOD

Follow the instructions for making a basic white dough. This is the technique that you'll use for all of your bakes, unless otherwise stated. So, combine your dry ingredients and set aside. Then add your yeast to the 320ml of water. Then slowly add the water and combine. Follow the water method and use all of the tests included in that section, to make sure your dough is good and has no knots or patches of flour.

Knead your dough, using the instructions included in the section on basic white dough.

Once you've kneaded once, the dough is ready for its first prove. Leave it for around 90 minutes. If you want to leave it for slightly longer, you can. The dough will start to move during that time.

Knead it for a second time. This is referred as 'knocking back' in other books. We're looking to do a series of turns and folds, which are outlined in the 'hints and tips' section on pages 48–49. You don't need to spend more than a minute doing that. Now leave it for its second rest, which should take around two hours.

The dough should now be ready to be divided, if you are making rolls or two 1lb loaves. Once you've completed your mould, leave the dough for its final prove. That should take 45 minutes.

Now you're ready to bake.

Bake in an oven preheated to 230C. If you're using a fan-assisted oven, bake at 220C. If you're using an Aga, bake at the highest setting.

Once you've baked for 10 minutes, drop the temperature by 10C for the rest of the bake.

Use the following baking times: for a 2lb loaf, 40–45 minutes; for a 1lb loaf, 25–30 minutes; for individual rolls 12–15 minutes.

WHOLEMEAL LOAF

LIKE the basic white loaf, a wholemeal should be part of any self-respecting baker's repertoire. There are a small number of key differences between the white loaf and the wholemeal. Before you begin to make your first loaf, read pages 38–39 on oils and fats. This loaf uses butter, which slightly changes the way it bakes.

INGREDIENTS

500g wholemeal flour
340ml water
8g salt
8g butter
5g fresh yeast
Extra water, up to 60ml, used in accordance with the water method

Makes one 2lb loaf, or two 1lb loaves

TIP: I'd advise around 380–400ml of water in total for this loaf, though start with 340ml and add the remainder using the water method. The quantity of water will vary, depending on the quality of your flour, atmospheric conditions and other variables.

Use unsalted butter, rather than salted. Salted butter will change both the flavour and the chemical composition. It could also slow the rate of development for your dough.

METHOD

Wholemeal dough will require more water than a basic white loaf, as the bran and fibre will absorb higher volumes when it rests. So use the water method to make sure your dough is slightly wetter and stickier than your basic white dough. As regards mixing and resting, your wholemeal dough requires a minimum of three rests. It may actually take four, if the flour has been stoneground.

Place your dry ingredients into the bowl and then add the butter. Mix, to soften the butter. Now add the yeasty water and follow the water method.

Knead once and then prove for at least 90 minutes, so that the bread starts to move.

Now turn and fold (knock back), for a minute, before leaving for its second rest. Leave it for around two hours.

Your bread should be turned and folded a second time and left for a third rest, of at least an hour – but more is fine. If you feel it needs a third fold and fourth rest, then go ahead. That allows the dough to develop.

Then it's time to divide and mould, after which you should leave your moulded loaf for 45 minutes, so that it's just starting to crown the tin. Then bake.

Place in a preheated conventional oven at 230C, a fan assisted oven at 220C or an Aga on the hottest setting. After 10 minutes, reduce the temperature by 10C for the rest of the bake.

Use the following baking times: for a 2lb loaf, 40–45 minutes; for a 1lb loaf, 25–30 minutes; for individual rolls 12–15 minutes.

Shropshire Crunch

THIS is a delicious loaf with a rich, malty flavour. It has a slight sweetness and the malted wheat flakes give it a delicious texture. Those that bake on the top will add a wonderful crunch to the loaf, hence the name. You need to use a combination of malts for the best effect.

INGREDIENTS

500g white flour
340ml water
100g malted wheat flakes
10g extratone malt
5g diastatic malt
8g salt
5g fresh yeast
Extra water, during water method: up to 40ml

Makes one 2lb loaf or two 1lb loaves

METHOD

As with all our bakes, use the water method (pages 24–25) and knead according to the techniques outlined in our basic dough (pages 26–29).

With the exception of the yeast and water, put all the ingredients into a bowl.

Add the yeast to the water and then mix. Now gradually add to the ingredients, to form your dough.

The diastatic and extratone malts will make this mix particularly tacky. Don't be put off by that. The dough will be very soft and it will absorb plenty of water while it is resting: 320ml should be pretty much what you want, though it could be a little more.

Once you've kneaded the dough, rest it for 90 minutes. Then turn and fold for a minute, before leaving for a further two hours. Give it a final knead before resting for a further hour.

Now divide and mould, then leave to prove for a final 45 minutes. Then bake.

Place in a preheated conventional oven at 230C, a fan assisted oven at 220C or an Aga on the hottest setting. After 10 minutes, reduce the temperature by 10C for the rest of the bake.

Use the following baking times: for a 2lb loaf, 40–45 minutes; for a 1lb loaf, 25–30 minutes; for individual rolls 12–15 minutes.

Shropshire Brown

THIS loaf combines a variety of malts and two different flours, in addition to wheat flakes. I start out with 340ml of water, but usually add another 30ml as I make my dough using the water method. I like to keep the salt ratio at around 2 per cent, so I've incorporated 10g for this bake. Our fermentation is slightly retarded by the use of malts, so the yeast percentage increases slightly to compensate for that. The result is a delightfully aromatic loaf.

INGREDIENTS

250g white flour
250g wholemeal flour
340ml water
70g malted wheat flakes
20g dark malt
10g extratone malt
10g diastatic malt
10g salt
7g yeast
Extra 30ml of water, to be incorporated during water method

Makes one 2lb loaf or two 1lb loaves

METHOD

Those who have followed the sequence of recipes, first mastering a white loaf before moving onto a basic wholemeal, will be pretty much up to speed with our method.

With the exception of the yeast and 340ml of water, place all of your ingredients into a bowl and mix round with your fingers, to combine. Remember, you don't want the yeasty water to come into contact with a high concentration of salt, or any other ingredient.

Now incorporate your yeasty water and start to form the dough.

You're following a similar process to the Shropshire Crunch, so knead the dough and then rest it for 90 minutes. Once it's started to move, turn and fold for a minute, before leaving for a further two hours. Now give it a final knead before resting for a further hour, then divide and mould, and leave to prove for a final 45 minutes. Then bake.

Place in a preheated conventional oven at 230C, a fan assisted oven at 220C or an Aga on the hottest setting. After 10 minutes, reduce the temperature by 10C for the rest of the bake.

Use the following baking times: for a 2lb loaf, 40–45 minutes; for a 1lb loaf, 25–30 minutes; for individual rolls 12–15 minutes.

Oatmill

THIS is a seriously thirsty dough because the oats soak up all the water. We've dropped the volume of flour a little, so that we don't make too much dough.

When your dough leaves the bowl, it should be as wet and sticky as possible. Don't worry if it seems too wet, the oats will drink the water as though it's the hottest day of the year.

Before you start, think about what happens when you make porridge. If you leave it in a bowl for a few minutes after you've made it, the oats will carry on drinking the milk and drying out the mix. That's what happens with this. So make sure you add enough water during the initial stages.

INGREDIENTS

400g white flour
100g rolled oats
50g pinhead oats
25g oatbran
340ml water
8g salt
5g yeast
Extra 60–70ml of water, to be incorporated during the water method

Makes one 2lb loaf or two 1lb loaves

METHOD

The water method comes into its own here. You will keep adding the water to rehydrate those oats and you'll need to take more time making your dough in the bowl. You really have to work this mix: make sure you're feeling strong because it'll give you a very good workout. The more time you take working the dough while it is in the bowl, the better it will be.

We're following the same method as our earlier bakes. So, with the exception of your yeast and water, add the ingredients into a bowl and mix them with your fingers. Now add the water and start to form the dough, adding additional water according to the water method.

Knead, then rest for 90 minutes. Fold and turn for a minute, then leave for a further two hours. Knead once more, then leave for a further hour. If you've time, knead and rest one final time, leaving it for a further hour. Finally, divide and mould, then leave to prove for a final 45 minutes.

Bake in a preheated conventional oven at 230C, a fan assisted oven at 220C or an Aga on the hottest setting. After 10 minutes, reduce the temperature by 10C for the rest of the bake.

Use the following baking times: for a 2lb loaf, 40–45 minutes; for a 1lb loaf, 25–30 minutes; for individual rolls 12–15 minutes.

SUNFLOWER AND GRAIN

THIS is a flavoursome bread that also has great texture. The beans and sunflower seeds have flavours of their own and also add extra texture to the finished bake. The beans will usually be bought dry and need to be rehydrated overnight. They need to be soaked so that they split their shells, soak up the water and double in size. They end up a nice yellow colour and give the dough plenty of flavour. Remember that by adding hydrated soya beans to the mix, you're adding extra water into your dough. For that reason, I bring down the volume of water to around 320ml, though, as ever, use the water method to make sure you are happy with your dough and it passes the regular tests.

INGREDIENTS

500g white flour
320ml water
60g sunflower seeds
30g soya beans (unsoaked weight), rehydrated overnight
8g salt
5g yeast

Makes one 2lb loaf or two 1lb loaves

METHOD

First weigh out your ingredients and add everything to the bowl, with the exception of the yeast and water. Mix the yeast and water and then incorporate into the bowl and start to form your dough. Make sure your beans and sunflower seeds are well incorporated. When you are testing your dough, using the pinch test, make sure you test a section of the dough that has no beans or seeds in it. The dough needs to be well worked because of the addition of the beans and seeds.

Now follow the standard method, giving your bread two rests: so, knead and leave for around 90 minutes, or a little longer. Turn and fold for a minute, then leave for a further two hours. Now divide and mould and leave for a further 45 minutes.

Now you're ready to bake.

Bake in an oven preheated to 230C. If you're using a fan-assisted oven, bake at 220C. If you're using an Aga, bake at the highest setting.

Once you've baked for 10 minutes, drop the temperature by 10C for the rest of the bake.

Use the following baking times: for a 2lb loaf, 40–45 minutes; for a 1lb loaf, 25–30 minutes; for individual rolls 12–15 minutes.

Honey and Sunflower

THIS has flavours that are evocative of summer and autumn. It is hearty and nutty and has excellent flavour. The sunflower seeds complement the slight honey flavour and it tastes great with slathers of butter.

INGREDIENTS

500g flour
320ml water
8g extratone malt
180g sunflower seeds
50g honey
8g yeast
5g salt

Makes one 2lb loaf or two 1lb loaves

METHOD

Mix your dry ingredients – flour, salt, malt and sunflower seeds. Then add your yeasty water. I recommend starting with 320ml, though you'll probably be able to add a further 20ml, using the water method. The honey is added later, because it slows the development of the gluten.

Follow the standard method, kneading your dough. It will be fairly rough and dry. Now work in the honey. Initially, it will be a horrible, sticky mess. Keep working it. We don't want the dough to be too stiff; the yeast has extra work to do to cope with the extra sugar in it. The malt will also soften the dough. When you've worked it to a good consistency, do your pinch test and check for your gluten window.

Give it a rest of around six minutes, then rework, then rest again before pulling it all together. When you are satisfied with the dough, prove for 90 minutes. Turn and fold, then prove for a further two hours. Don't be surprised if it's sluggish to start with; that will be because of the honey. If you need to leave it a little longer, do so.

Divide and mould the dough and put it into your tin. If you want more texture, roll in a few seasame seeds. Prove for 45 minutes and bake, adding steam into the oven. Bake at 230C, turning down to 220C after 10 minutes, with 40–45 minutes for a large loaf, 25–30 minutes for two 1lb loaves or 12–15 minutes for rolls.

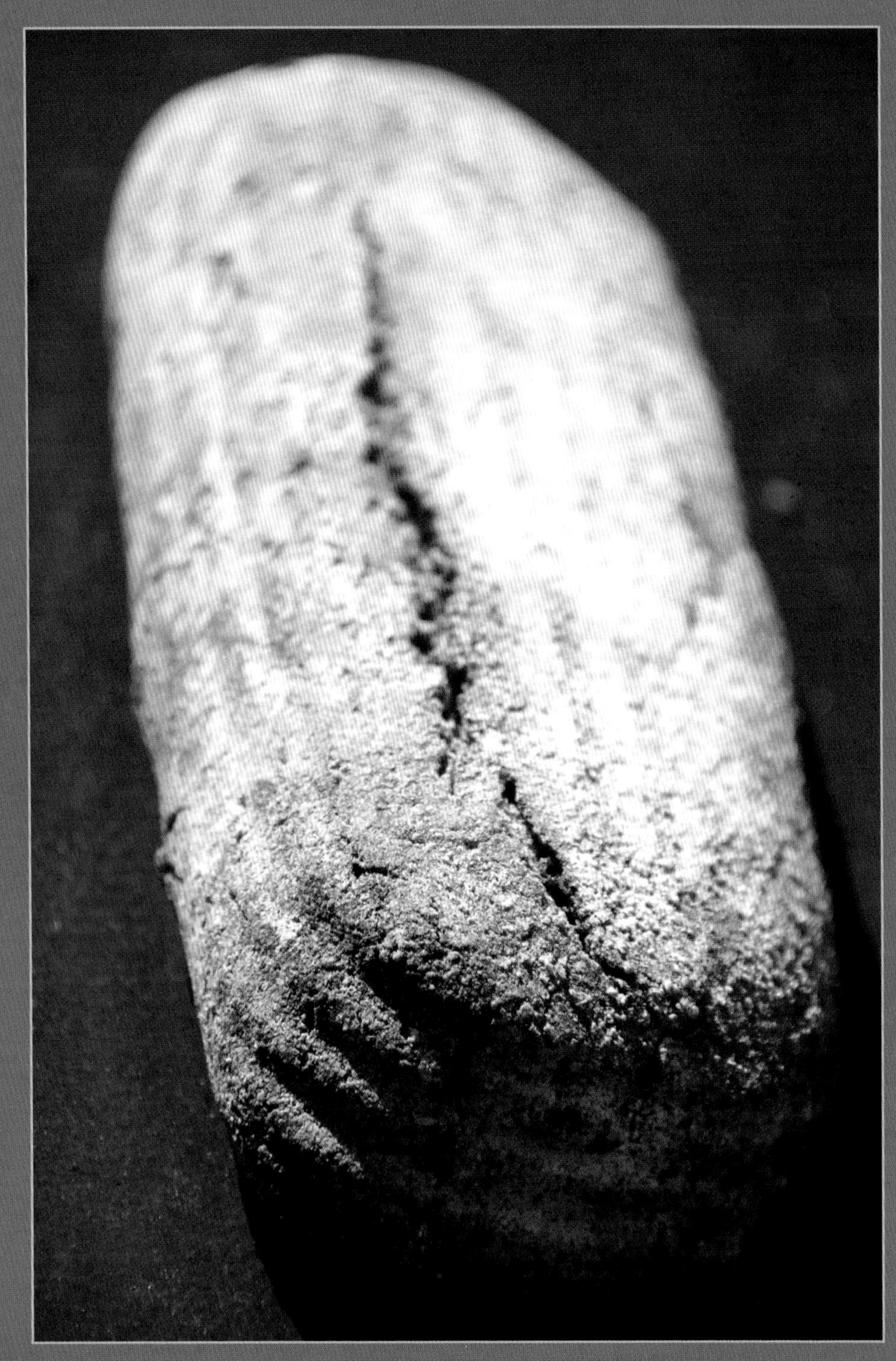

RYE

RYE bread breaks all the rules and regulations with regard to resting and gluten. The reason for that is simple: rye flour doesn't contain any wheat, so there's no gluten in it. It's a totally different dough. Rye is worked in the bowl, not on the table. Since there is no gluten to absorb the water, the dough doesn't become as tight. Rather than making an elastic dough, the dough is rather like a paste.

INGREDIENTS

500g rye flour
340ml water
3g yeast
8g salt

METHOD

Mix the salt and rye flour, then incorporate the yeasted water. Work into the mix. Rye flour is quite thirsty so will absorb plenty of water. Rye flour also tends to absorb more water after mixing, so make sure it's not too dry, otherwise the loaf will be too dense and heavy.

Work in extra water, if needs be, using the water method. You are looking for a dough that is soft enough to work with a wooden spoon: you almost need to be able to 'paste it' along the side of the bowl. We don't give this the regulation five/six minute rests, as we do with most breads. We just keep mixing until we are happy that the water has gone in. It should feel soft and a little bit slimey. Once you've reached that point, pull the dough together with a plastic scraper and allow to prove in the bowl. It needs two hours for the first prove.

Give it a little turn and fold – literally ten seconds will do, don't be vigorous – then leave it for two more hours.

Flour the table with rye flour, tip it out and divide it into two. Shape with a very loose bloomer mould [*see pages 30–33*], then pop into a long proving basket. Make sure the mould is well floured. Now pop the dough in upside down, so that the seam faces up. When you finish proving, after an hour or longer, you'll tip it out and the seam will be facing downwards. Don't expect massive things – it won't increase too much in size. Place on a preheated baking tray. Add a little steam to the oven and bake at 220C for 35–40 minutes. It takes a lot to bake through and not be raw in the middle. Rye will give you a dense loaf; don't expect a massive jump when it bakes.

Spelt Wholemeal

THIS loaf is almost identical to our wholemeal loaf. The spelt wholemeal flour will give you a fairly soft mix but don't worry about that – that's just the way it is. When you're making this for the first time, you might want to bake it in a tin. Once you're happy, you can progress to baking it in more complex shapes on a baking tray. When you move to baking it on a tray, make sure you double mould, so that you can really tighten up the dough and get it into a reasonably firm state.

INGREDIENTS

500g spelt wholemeal flour
340ml water
8g salt
8g butter
5g fresh yeast
Extra water, up to 40ml, used in accordance with the water method

Makes one 2lb loaf or two 1lb loaves

METHOD

The spelt wholemeal flour will absorb higher volumes of water than a basic white loaf, though not quite as much as the wholemeal flour. You'll probably be able to give it one rest fewer than for your wholemeal loaf – so give it three rests, instead of four.

You're probably accustomed to the method by now, so let's whizz through it:

With the exception of the yeast and water, place your ingredients into the bowl and mix them together. Start to incorporate the water, following the water method, adding up to 40ml more than your initial 340ml of yeast solution.

Knead once and then prove for at least 90 minutes, so that the bread starts to move.

Now turn and fold, for a minute, before leaving for its second rest. Leave for two hours. Turn and fold a second time then rest for a further hour before dividing, moulding and leaving to prove for 90 minutes.

Then bake in a preheated conventional oven at 230C, a fan assisted oven at 220C or an Aga on the hottest setting. After 10 minutes, reduce the temperature by 10C for the rest of the bake.

Use the following baking times: for a 2lb loaf, 40–45 minutes; for a 1lb loaf, 25–30 minutes; for individual rolls 12–15 minutes.

Pepper Bread

THIS is one of my most attractive breads. The vibrant reds, yellows and greens of peppers can be contrasted with chopped chives, and the dough bakes to a beautiful golden brown. Dried herbs work well with this; they avoid adding any excess moisture and have an intense flavour.

INGREDIENTS

500g flour
340ml water
8g salt
5g salt
10g dried mixed herbs (when you dry herbs the flavour intensifies)
40ml olive oil
1 pepper (red, green or yellow, or a mixture)
60g sundried tomatoes, in oil
Chives and paprika, to decorate

METHOD

Chop the sundried tomatoes very finely. They ought to have a little oil to keep them moist; you don't want them to be too dry. Take a single pepper, cut it in half, deseed it and then cut one half into fine strips. Put the other half to one side. Then cut those strips into small dice, and set aside.

Put your dry ingredients into a bowl, including the salt, flour and dry herbs. Mix with your fingers and then add the yeasty water to start to make a dough. Once you're happy with the dough, add the olive oil. If you need to spot a little extra water in, using the water method, then do so. You may be able to add up to 40ml (I call it 'just-in-case water' – it's there just in case you need it).

Add your sundried tomatoes and work those through the dough. Turn the dough onto the table and start to knead. Give it two rests of five to six minutes, then work in your chopped half-pepper. It should be nicely dispersed. Pull it together and let it rest, the same as for a basic white dough.

Divide it into three equal parts and use the moulding method for the small batch [*pages 30-33*]. Leave to rest for 10 to 15 minutes.

Now, oil the table. Using a scraper, take the dough and vigorously chop all the way through it. Then put the dough pieces into a sponge tin, measuring 15–20cm. Sprinkle the top with paprika. Prove then until the dough is coming over the top of the tin: half an hour should do it.

Take the other half of the pepper, deseed and thinly slice, it, then scatter lightly over the dough. Bake at 230C for ten minutes then turn it down to 220C. You're looking to cook it for 20 minutes. Drizzle it with olive oil when it comes out, then sprinkle chopped chives on top to decorate.

bread2bake

Soda Bread

THERE are numerous variations of sodabread. Ireland, Scotland, Australia and Serbia all have unique recipes. The ingredients include buttermilk and bicarbonate of soda, which react to form tiny bubbles of carbon dioxide.

INGREDIENTS

500g plain flour
2 tsp bicarbonate of soda (you could use baking powder)
1 tsp fine sea salt
Approximately 400ml buttermilk or live yoghurt
A little milk will be needed to get a nice sticky consistency

METHOD

Sift the flour and bicarbonate of soda into a large mixing bowl and stir in the salt. Make a well in the centre and pour in the buttermilk, stirring as you go. If necessary, add a tablespoon or two of milk to bring the mixture together; it should form a soft, sticky dough. Do all of your mixing in the bowl because the dough will be too soft to work on the table. Make sure all your flour and liquid are combined, and work together for one or two minutes. You're not looking for the kind of smooth, elastic dough you get with a yeast-based bread.

Now tip it onto a well-floured work surface. Divide into three equal pieces, roughly 300g each. Loosely work into a round shape. Put the round of dough on a lightly floured baking sheet. Push down with your fingers lightly, to spread out the dough a little. Dust generously with flour.

Mark a deep cross in it with a sharp, serrated knife, cutting about two-thirds of the way through the loaf, or use your plastic or metal scraper. Put it in an oven preheated to 220C and bake for 35 minutes, until the loaf sounds hollow when tapped underneath. Cool on a wire rack if you like a crunchy crust, or wrap in a clean tea towel if you prefer a soft crust.

TIP: Soda bread is best eaten while still warm, spread with salty butter and/or a dollop of your favourite jam. But if you have some left over the next day, it makes great toast.

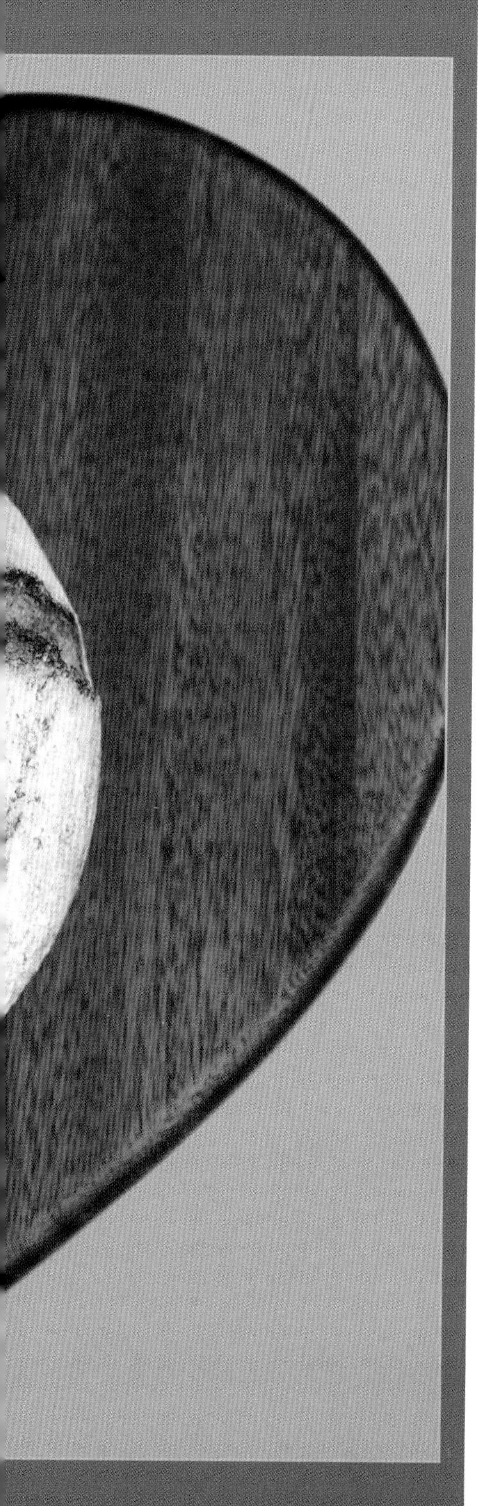

SOURDOUGH

MAKING sourdough is possibly the most satisfying way of making bread. It is, however, the most time-consuming, the most technical and not something that should be undertaken lightly. If you want to bake this type of bread, you first need to acknowledge that it requires a major commitment.

We have previously likened breadmaking to the creation of a life, which passes through various stages including infancy, adolescence and maturity. If you are making sourdough, you are entering into a further stage: marriage. Sourdough requires a lifelong commitment. Once you have created your starter culture, you are creating the food that will create more and more bread.

The care and attention that you give the starter will have a bearing on the breads that you make. If you neglect the starter, it will die and be of no use. Look after your starter and it will give you great-tasting, great-looking bread. If I've not already put you off then it's time to get started!

A sourdough is a dough containing a lactobacillus culture (the bacteria), which gives it its defining sour tang. It also contains natural leavening micro-organisms (natural yeasts), which are found not only in the atmosphere but are also present within the flour that we create the culture with.

Just to clarify, the 'starter' is the instrument that is going to prove and ferment our dough. This negates the need to use any fresh yeast at all.

1
1a
Not all starters will look exactly the same, but these pictures give you a good guide.
2
2a

GETTING STARTED

The first thing you need to do is to create your culture. We are about to embark on a process that will take between 10 and 14 days.

DAY 1

220ml water (approximately 25C)
180g white flour

Mix together to form a paste, place in a container and close the lid. Please note that at times the lid will need to be loosened to release some of the carbon dioxide created. This will be created as the culture develops. (*See pictures* **1** *and* **1a**).

DAYS 2 AND 3

The culture now starts to evolve and begins to grow. It will form bubbles, which will start to break on the surface. It should give you a yeasty aroma at this point. Some people chose to use grapes to enhance the fermentation; those who do will get lighter and frothier bubbles. (*See pictures* **2** *and* **2a**).

DAY 4

It is now time to refresh the culture and to do this you add the following:

60ml water
50g white flour

Add those ingredients to your existing culture and mix together. The culture at this point may have started to deflate and begin to discolour a little.

We are refreshing the starter to keep the balance between the acidity of the cultures and the yeasts present. If the acidity is too high, it will kill the yeast. So we are helping our culture by adding flour and water. The flour feeds the yeast due to the presence of sugars that are found in the flour's starch. The water allows us to keep the culture at the right consistency. The more water we add, the more liquid the culture will be; the less water we add, the firmer it will be. (*See pictures* **3** *and* **3a** *overleaf*).

DAYS 5-9

There isn't much to do to the culture at this point, although you should check it every day to see how it is changing. It is possible that the culture may separate, forming a yellowish liquid on top. If that happens, just pour the liquid away. It could also form a mould over the top. If it does that, remove it immediately and replenish with 60g flour and 60ml of water. The mould may be evidence of an imbalance in the bacteria and yeast. All being well, the unpleasant smell of a young culture should be replaced by a yeasty aroma that you might have smelled on days two and three.

DAY 10

Today is the day when your starter becomes a culture, and an intense feeding programme begins.

Weigh out 400g of the culture and discard the rest. We are now looking to build up its strength. The regular feeding distinguishes a culture from our starter.

DAYS 10-14

First feeding. Take the 400g of starter and add to that:

60ml water
50g rye flour (we are going to introduce rye at times to change the starter a little bit)

Second feeding six hours later:

120ml water
110g white flour

Third feeding six hours later:

240ml water
220g white flour

You need to do this at a time that allows you

3
3a
4
4a

to attend to each process. For example, start at 8am, then again at 2pm, then again at 8pm.

It is important before you begin each day's feeding to pour away all but 400g of your starter, otherwise you will have enough starter to fill a bath. Contine this feeding process until day 15, by which point your starter will be ready. (*See pictures* **4** *and* **4a**).

Notice the lovely honeycomb texture of your starter and the active bubbles it should have. Your starter is now ready to be made into bread.

SOURDOUGH: INGREDIENTS

300g white flour
100g wholemeal spelt
50g rye
150g starter
6g salt
300ml water, which will probably rise to 350ml

METHOD

Add all of your dry ingredients into the bowl, work in the salt and add your starter.

Add three quarters of your water and begin to work the mixture in the bowl. Use the water method from this point on, gently adding your water and mixing. The use of rye and spelt flours will alter the feel of the dough slightly. However, you must make sure your dough is well hydrated. Do the usual tests in the bowl, eg, the pinch test.

Bring the tacky, sticky dough out onto the table and begin to knead. Give your dough three six-minute rests during the mixing process. Pull your dough together and do the regular tests. Remember, the rye and wholemeal spelt will slightly affect the gluten window.

When you are happy with your dough, oil the bowl, place the dough inside and cover. The proving time in its bulk state should be anything up to 10 hours.

If you are making sourdough during the day, put turns and folds onto it every three hours. If you are holding overnight, give it a fermentation of between two and three hours, then turn and fold before covering and placing in the fridge. When you wake up, bring it out, turn and fold, then allow a further two hours fermentation at room temperature.

Now flour the table, tip out the dough and divide into two equal parts. Flour your proving basket and use either bloomer- or batch-moulding techniques, depending on the shape of the proving basket. Place your dough in upside down with the crease facing upwards. Cover and prove for a final time for another two hours.

Half an hour before baking, preheat the oven to 220C and pop in a baking tray or baking stone. When the tray or stone is very hot, gently turn the bread onto the baking tray and put a single cut into the top of your loaf with your lame. Now put it into the oven with a little steam and bake for 35–40 minutes.

As regards your starter, always remember to replace the amount you took out and continue to keep up the regular feedings. If you are not using your starter for a prolonged length of time, keep it in the fridge and bring it out the day before to begin feeding again.

Sourdough is a very testing recipe, but once you can master it you can call yourself an advanced baker.

CIABATTA

CIABATTA has a delightfully open texture and combines a crunchy exterior with a soft, spongy interior. You can make them in a variety of sizes: a small loaf of ciabatta is called panino – the plural is the now-ubiquitous Panini.

INGREDIENTS

400g ciabatta rustica
100g durum semolina
8g salt
2g fresh yeast
300ml water, first mix
Up to 150ml water, second mix

Makes three to six ciabatta, depending on the size that you roll them

METHOD

If you are unable to obtain ciabatta rustica flour, then substitute with Italian '00'. It will produce a similar bake. You need to mix your ciabatta dough twice before leaving to prove. During your first mix, add 300ml of yeasty water to the dry ingredients. Start to work it. It will be a very thirsty dough. Once you've got a very sticky dough rest for five or six minutes, then chop it into four.

Now start your second mix. Start to squeeze the dough with the water. Once it's absorbed as much as possible, put it back on the table and work. You will create a very sticky dough. Give it another five-minute rest, then put it back into the bowl. Chop it into four again, working it in separate pieces. The stronger the gluten becomes the more water it will take. We are looking to get up to 450ml of water into the dough, so it needs a lot of work. If you're a little light on the total water, at 425ml, for instance, don't worry.

That mix will give you a nice open crumb with a crisp top. When you are happy with your dough, oil the bowl, pop it inside and give it a 90-minute prove. Turn and fold, then give it a 90-minute prove, again turn and fold and rest for an hour.

Now flour the table well with a mix of white flour and semolina. Tip your dough out and divide it into three equal strips. Then put two baking trays, or baking stones, into a preheated oven, at 210C. If you can use flat ones, without sides, they are the best. The objective is to cook it from beneath, as well as from the top and sides.

While the trays are heating, leave the dough to rest for about 30 minutes. Now pull the ends of the ciabattas a little, so that they stretch. Place onto the trays and bake. Don't put any steam in the oven; the bread is already generously hydrated and extra water will make it rubbery. Give them around 25–30 minutes for standard-sized ciabatta.

FOCACCIA

THIS flat, oven-baked Italian bread is wonderfully light and incredibly versatile. It is made using a high-gluten flour, with salt and olive oil to season. It can be flavoured with a wide variety of ingredients; you could try sundried tomato, caramelised onion, goat's cheese and rosemary, or sea salt.

INGREDIENTS

FIRST MIX
200g Tipo '00' flour
150ml water, tepid
1.5g fresh yeast

SECOND MIX
100g durum semolina flour
5g sea salt/salt flakes
20ml water
15ml olive oil

This makes one tray, measuring approximately 20cm × 30cm

METHOD

First mix. Take 120ml of your water in a jug, add the yeast and stir to disperse. Weigh the flour into a mixing bowl and add the water/yeast solution. Slowly begin to work the ingredients together by gently folding the flour over until it begins to form a dough. It should have a soft, almost wet consistency. Don't be afraid to add the remaining water, if you need to. Once mixed, cover and rest for an hour-and-a-half.

Second mix. Add the semolina flour to the rested dough in the bowl. Dissolve the salt in the water then add it to the dough. Add the olive oil. Mix into the already proved dough in your bowl. Care should be taken while the flour is taken into the dough. When you have completed the process, empty the dough onto the table and begin to knead until it is developed and a gluten window is visible. Cover and leave to rest for two hours, then turn and fold, and prove for another two hours.

Turn and fold then oil your baking tray and press the focaccia onto it. Leave it to prove for an hour.

Add your toppings: that could be red onion, rosemary and rock salt; tomato with basil and mozzarella; or a different combination.

Bake at 230C for 10 minutes, then turn the oven down to 220C and cook for a further five to 10 minutes. The dough should start to pull away from the side of the tray and it should have a springy, spongy texture, without being hard-baked. It needs good colour.

Stromboli

THIS bread is a sexy little fella. Packed with flavour, it oozes melted cheese from either end and looks absolutely stunning. It's a real hit with the customers. The moment they see it, they want it – it flies off the shelves. It's the sort of bread that you can't put down. People think they'll just have one slice – then end up eating the lot.

INGREDIENTS

125g tipo '00' flour
125g ciabatta rustica
50g durum semolina
5g salt
1.5g fresh yeast
180ml water
Additional 20ml water using the water method
15ml olive oil
Generous handful of grated mozzarella
Generous handful of grated applewood smoked cheddar
3 shallots, finely chopped
Basil, roughly chopped
1 clove of garlic, crushed
A pinch of sea salt

METHOD

This is a simple all-in-one recipe. First add your dry ingredients to the bowl, then follow the water method, adding in 180ml of yeasty solution.

You're looking for a nice, soft sticky dough. Work it on the table. Once the dough has taken on the water, add in the oil. Continue to work it until the oil is fully incorporated. Now add in up to 20ml of extra water, using the water method.

Give it two rests of five minutes and work the graininess of durum semolina away as best you can. It won't all disappear. Prove for two hours, turn and fold, then prove for a further two-and-a-half hours.

Take the dough out and put it onto the table. It should be nice and soft and you'll be able to pin it out into an A4-sized piece using your fingers. Make sure you have a nice little dusting of flour, or durum semolina, underneath.

Now you're ready to add your filling, including grated mozzarella cheese, grated smoked applewood cheese, shallots finely chopped, basil roughly chopped, garlic and little pinch of sea salt.

Now roll it up. Pull the dough back over the top and push it down. Always roll towards you from top to bottom. You need a little pressure to keep the filling in. Once it's rolled, cut it in half. Take a sharp knife and with the point poke a hole half the way along and stick a piece of rosemary inside. Give the loaf a little stretch and place it on the baking tray. Coat liberally with olive oil, sprinkle with black pepper, cover and prove for an hour. It should be 50 per cent bigger, rather than doubled in size. Then bake for 20–22 minutes at 230C for the first 10 minutes, then 220C.

TIP: A different filling might be prosciutto ham with sundried tomatoes. Use your imagination!

Rustic French Country Loaf

THIS delicious and attractive loaf is made using poolish (see pages 40–41 for further information on poolish). It's a stand-out bake that gives you the opportunity to demonstrate your skill as a baker. You'll need to start this loaf a day before you bake it.

INGREDIENTS

Flour mix
455g French white flour
50g rye flour (light)
20g extratone malt flour

For poolish
175g flour mix
175ml water
1g yeast

Further mix
Remaining 350g of flour mix
180ml water, plus up to 50ml extra using the water method
8g salt
2g yeast

METHOD

Stage 1. First make your flour mix. Blend the three ingredients so that the malt and rye discolour the white flour, giving it a greyish appearance.

Weigh 175g of the grey flour mix to make your poolish.

Stage 2. Now mix your poolish. Cover and allow to stand at room temperature for 60–90 minutes until little bubbles appear on the surface. Place in the fridge for between 12 and 14 hours.

Remove the poolish from the fridge and allow to stand at room temperature for an hour.

Stage 3. We want this dough to be well hydrated and quite sticky before we bring it out onto the table. When kneading, you may want to put a little oil onto your hands to help you. Give three rests of five minutes during mixing. Your gluten window may be slightly less opaque than normal, due to the presence of rye flour. The dough should still be smooth and almost glossy. Complete the tests, then cover. Prove for 90 minutes then turn and fold. Prove for a further 90 minutes then turn and fold, before proving for a further 90 minutes.

Flour your table well with a mix of white flour and rye. Gently tip your dough onto the flour and also flour the top of the dough. Using the plastic scraper, divide evenly into two. Cover with a plastic bag.

Place a baking tray into an oven preheated to 210C until it is hot. Remove the tray and quickly place your loaves directly onto the tray. Bake for 40 minutes with no steam.

PAN CASERO WITH ROSEMARY AND RAISINS

PAN Casero is also known as Spanish house bread and can be made without the addition of rosemary and raisins. One of my favourite recipes features Pan Casero that is plaited into a large circle; it follows the same recipe, with the omission of the rosemary and raisin, and is one of the most visually stunning breads imaginable. This deliciously light loaf has great texture and taste.

INGREDIENTS

450g white flour
50g spelt
340ml water
20ml olive oil
8g salt
5g yeast
1 egg
20g raisin
2–3 sprigs of rosemary, stems removed, roughly chopped
10g malted wheat flakes
10g sesame seeds
10g rolled oats

Makes three small loaves

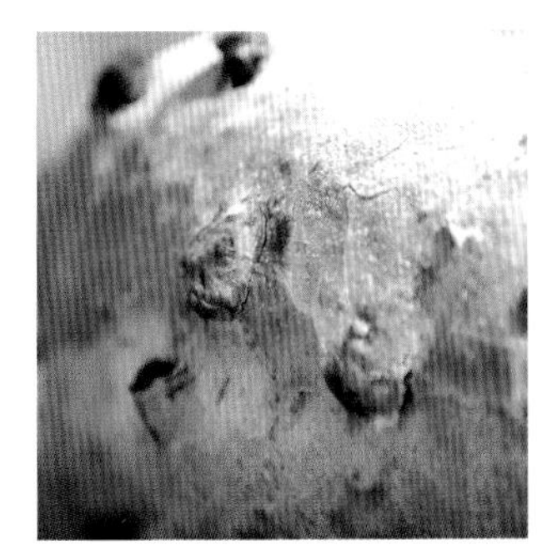

METHOD

Weigh your flour, salt, egg, malted wheat flakes, sesame seeds and rolled oats into the bowl. Work it together so that the seeds and the flakes are evenly dispersed. Add the yeast to the water, mix, then begin to add the yeasty water to the flour using the water method. Once your water is in, carry out your normal checks to make sure there are no dry patches of flour. Now add the olive oil and work in. If your dough is sticky, bring it onto the table and start working. Give two rests of five minutes, as normal. Your gluten window won't be too transparent, but carry out your tests and check for elasticity. When you're happy, soak your raisins for three minutes in hot water, drain and add rosemary to them. Chop your dough into four and place back in the bowl. Add rosemary and raisins to dough to suit, but do not add more than you have soaked. If you would like to add a little more rosemary, go ahead.

Place the dough into the bowl and rest for 90 minutes, turn and fold, then rest for another two hours. Divide into three and mould as a 'bloomer'. Prove for a further 45 minutes then bake at 220C for 25–30 minutes.

TIP: For something different chop the dough piece into two. Roll out each piece to 25–30cm. Attach ends at the top and simply plait all way down. Then take the plait and join into a ring, place onto baking tray, and prove for 45 minutes. Dust with sieved flour and bake at 220C for 20 minutes.

French Rustic Baguette

THIS is a classic bake that uses poolish, rather than a standard yeast solution. Refer to the poolish table below for further details. It uses an overnight process and produces a bake that will make you the envy of your friends.

INGREDIENTS

Poolish mix
175g flour
175ml water
1g yeast

Second mix
350g flour
8g salt
2g yeast
150ml water, plus additional using the water method

METHOD

Poolish mix. Mix together as described on page 40–41. Allow the poolish to sit for 60–90 minutes. It should be covered until you see little bubbles appearing on the surface. Then place it in the fridge overnight for 12–14 hours.

Second mix. Give your poolish an hour at room temperature and then begin to mix with the flour and further water. Keep the dough sticky and tacky. Give it three short rests of five or six minutes during mixing. Move onto your tests and then cover and prove for 90 minutes. Turn and fold, prove for a further 90 minutes, then turn and fold once more. Prove for an hour then divide into four equal sizes, weighing approximately 220g each. Loosely pull together into a tin shape, cover and rest for 15 minutes.

Flour a surface well, take your dough piece and fold over top-to-bottom, to create a baguette mould. Roll that through the flour, covering it all over. Place on a baking tray. Crease the sides and then cover for the final time, proving for 45 minutes. Bake with a little steam from a spray bottle at 215C for 20–25 minutess until golden and crisp.

Brioche

BRIOCHE is a deliciously buttery, highly enriched dough that hails from France. It has a light and fluffy texture and a dark, flaky crust. It's delicious. It can be enriched in a number of ways: this version uses plenty of butter, sugar and eggs to give it a rich, luxurious texture and taste. Brioche can be baked with fruit, chocolate chips or other additions. It can also be eaten with sweet or savoury accompaniments, from foie gras and sausage to beef en croute, or it can be eaten sweet with tea.

INGREDIENTS

500g French white flour, preferably T45
200g unsalted butter, diced
100ml water
Extra 20ml 'just-in-case' water
60g sugar
4 eggs
7g salt
5g yeast

METHOD

Add all ingredients into bowl, except the butter and yeasted water. Sift by hand. Add your yeasted water. We don't need to stick rigidly to the water method here and you can add all of the 100ml in one go for this dough, because a lot of the moisture will come from adding the butter.

Begin to blend water into the rest of the ingredients. This dough will feel quite dry and rough as we have at this point under-hydrated our dough. However, if the dough has a lot of hard dryness then just spot a little extra water in until all flour is incorporated. At this stage, we are not looking for a dough that is wet and sticky.

Once your dough has formed it should look very rough. Begin to work in some of your butter, around a third. If you like, you can first cut up your rough dough into four quarters and then pop it back into the bowl (**1**, *over*), so that it has a greater surface area. I always find it best to incorporate the butter in three stages. Never try to add all of the butter at once because the dough simply won't take it. Do this in your mixing bowl, rather than on the table. Once the first third of your butter has started to go into your dough (**2**), begin to add the next few lumps of butter, and repeat the process until all the butter is worked in.

At this point your dough will now be very wet and sticky (**3**). Don't worry, this is completely normal. As you continue to work in the bowl the dough will begin to pull together. It will be soft and will have started to take on a yellow colour.

Now it's time to bring the dough out onto the table. You do not need to flour the table because the butter in the dough will ensure it does not stick. Take the dough and begin to stretch it and work it on the table. You will need to use your plastic scraper to help you get any excess dough off the table. The smoother and silkier the dough gets, the less you will need to use your scraper. ➤

1
2
3
4

The brioche requires a great deal of work and it will require a minimum of three rests during the mixing – you'll probably require a similar number yourself!

As you work your dough, you will notice that it becomes smoother and develops a nice sheen. Once your dough has got to that point it is ready to begin its rest and proof (**4**). Pull the dough together, dust it with a little flour and place it into a polythene bag or container with a secure lid. Now pop it in the fridge for a minimum of 12 hours. It can be left for longer – up to 36 hours. When you take your dough out of the fridge give it an hour at room temperature so that it can begin to soften. Always keep it covered.

As the dough begins to soften you can divide it into desired shapes and weights; either in 1lb tins, a brioche tin, or little rolls. The dough will then need to be proved again before baking. Leave it for approximately two to three hours. Again, make sure your bread is covered but don't try to add heat to your breads as this will just melt the butter and it will run out of your dough.

Once your brioche has increased in size at least 50 per cent lightly brush it with an egg wash, being careful not to push too hard when applying the wash. Then bake. Cook it at 150C for a conventional oven. A 1lb loaf should take 40 minutes and small rolls will take 15–20 minutes. The bake needs to be low and slow due to the butter, egg and sugar content. If your oven is too hot your brioche will just burn.

Croissants

RICH, buttery, flaky croissants are a real treat. Bakers have made them since the Middle Ages and possibly since even earlier. They have long been a staple of French life and are among the most distinctive items of French food. Croissants came under attack in the late 1970s when factories began to churn out frozen, pre-formed varieties. But I'm a great advocate of doing things properly. This recipe is relatively straightforward and the joy you'll get from making and baking your own croissants is immeasurable. They add a real wow factor to your table: when you tell people you've been making your own croissants they'll be completely impressed.

INGREDIENTS

500g white French flour T45
250ml water (you can use a mixture of 150ml double cream and 100ml water)
Extra 20ml of water, to be incorporated using the water method
70g sugar
40g yeast
20g salt
250g unsalted butter

METHOD

Croissant-making is time-consuming but ultimately very rewarding. To begin with, weigh your flour, salt and sugar into a bowl and, as highlighted in our mixing section, work those three ingredients together. Start to work the yeasty water in. If you are using the cream/water mix, then put all the water in and begin to add cream. Whichever variation you have chosen, you will still need to use the water method to make sure your dough is correctly hydrated. With this recipe you should be looking at adding up to 20ml of extra water.

When you are happy with your dough, bring it out onto the table and work it. Give it two rests during the mixing process, making sure you carry out your tests to ensure a perfect dough. The dough will be a little tighter than basic bread dough but you still need to have the elasticity and a gluten window.

If you are making the dough with the mix that uses the cream, you will achieve a better gluten window than if you are not. The fat will help the dough to create an exceptional gluten window.

Once you are happy with the dough, pull it all together and put it back in the bowl. Brush a little oil over the top, cover and rest for 30–45 minutes. Now take out your dough and roll out into a rectangle about 1cm thick. Place in the freezer for 20–30 minutes.

Now take your butter from the fridge. It should be firm. Don't be worried about smacking it with the rolling pin, to help it to soften. Using a floured piece of silicone or baking paper, wrap up the butter and use your rolling pin to create a square (**1**, *over*), then place that in the freezer for the remainder of the time that the dough is in there.

Bring both your dough and butter out of freezer, brush

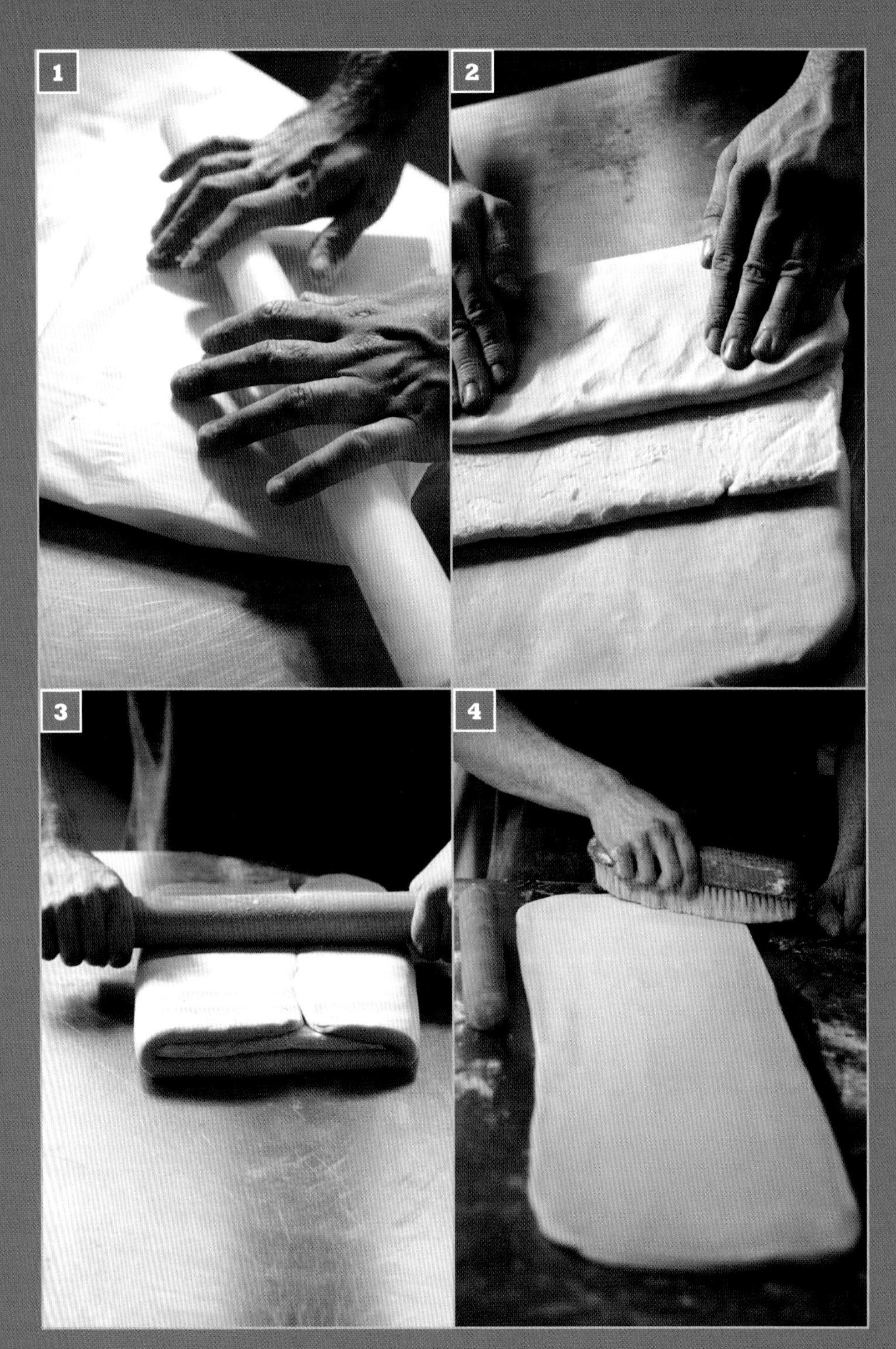
1
2
3
4

off any flour and place your butter in the middle third of the dough. Fold over the other thirds so they meet in the middle (**2**). Turn the dough through 90 degrees so the crease is running vertically from top to bottom. Begin rolling out to extend your rectangle (**3**). Work it away from you, and get your dough to a thickness of roughly ½–1cm. You then need to give your dough a book turn. Do this by folding both edges in until they meet in the middle. Give that a little roll, to even everything up. Then fold one half onto the other to end up with something that looks a little like a book. Once again, flatten this a little with the rolling pin making the rectangle about half as big again.

If weather conditions or your kitchen are hot, you may need to refirm your dough by putting it back into the freezer for 15 minutes, just to make sure the butter stays firm. The objective is to work the fat and dough together to create what is called lamination. Lamination is easily understood: when you break into a croissant, you see lots of thin, individual layers – that's lamination. The process involves the layering of dough and fat. Getting that right will give a light, open layered crumb on the inside of the croissant. As the fat boils and dissolves it leaves behind the dough layer so the croissant seems to have lots of individual rings inside, almost like a tree.

Now carry on with your rolling. You should start with the sealed end on the right-hand side and the folds on the left. Begin to roll this out and elongate the rectangle.

Now we're ready for our last fold. Once the dough is rolled to roughly double the size, mark halfway and simply fold in two. You should have a sealed end at the bottom and folds on the other three sides. Again give the dough a little roll to even it up and place back into the freezer for 20–30 minutes.

Take your dough out of the freezer and roll into a nice, even square. Remember to always brush off any excess flour (**4**). Then, along the length of the dough fold in half to make a divide. Unfold again and cut along that line to give you two separate halves. Mark diagonals from top to bottom to make triangles and this will be the basis of your croissant (you would cut into rectangles for pains au chocolat).

The final proof can be quite long, anything up to 2-2½ hours.

Now form your croissants (**5–9**). Roll them up by

5
6
7
8

9

pinching at the tip of the triangle and rolling the thicker side forwards with the palm of your hand.

Egg wash your croissant before you set them to prove and make sure you keep them covered. Your croissants should double in size. Egg wash once more, after they've proved.

Now bake. Set your oven to 210C and bake for 20–25 minutes. Turn your oven down to 200C after 10 minutes to allow the croissants to bake nicely without burning.

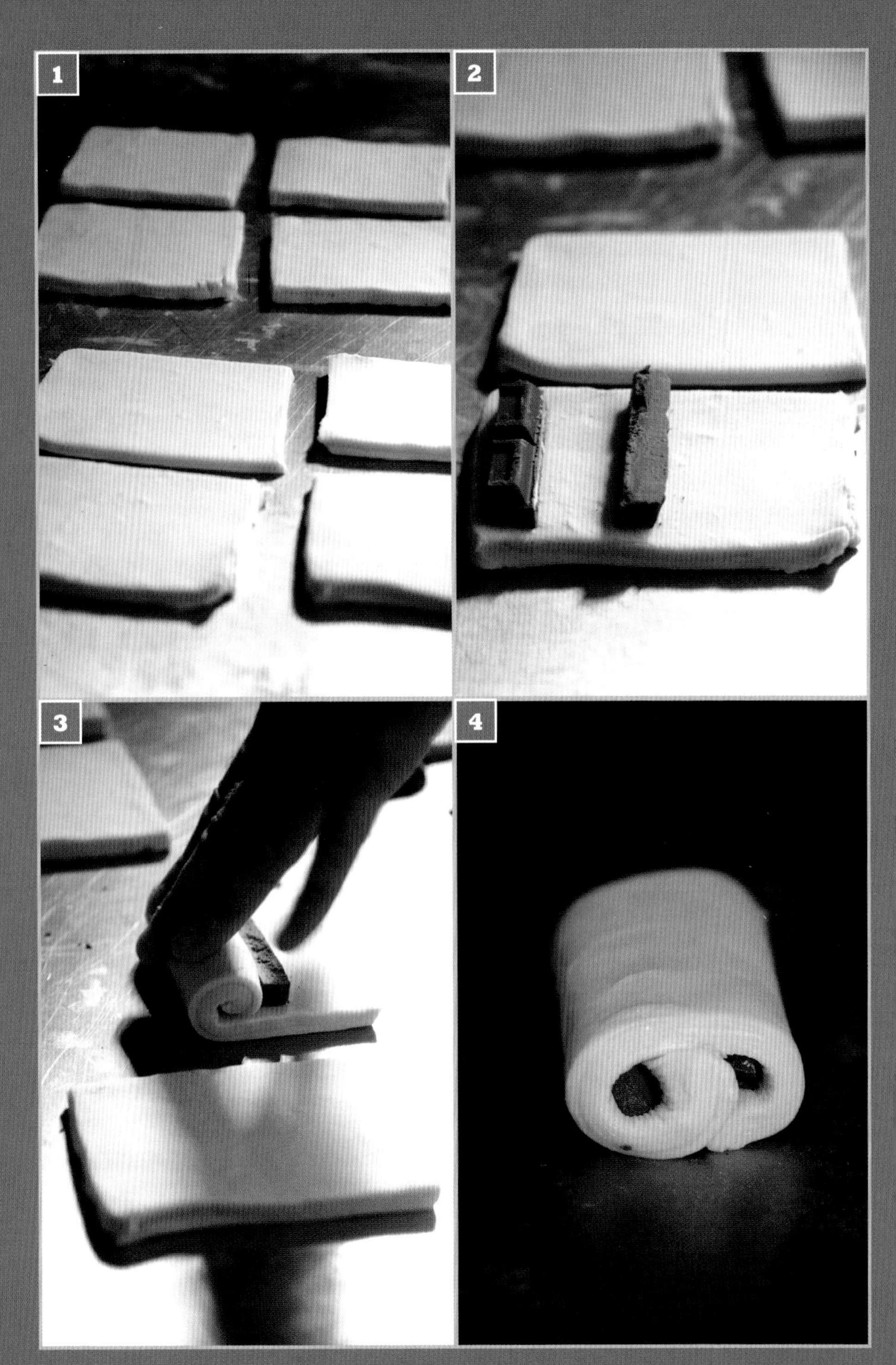
1
2
3
4

Pains au Chocolat

THIS recipe uses precisely the same dough that we've used for croissants. Refer to pages 100–105 for the full recipe.

INGREDIENTS

See page 101

METHOD

The difference between this method and the one for croissants is that here you place chocolate sticks onto the pastry, then fold it over widthways, rather than lengthways. There are numerous suppliers selling pain au chocolat chocolate sticks. However, you don't have to buy those. Much higher quality chocolate is available in bar form. It's also fun to experiment with different varieties.

Pain au chocolat is even easier to make than croissants.

Simply take a quantity of your croissant dough and give it a little stretch, if necessary, to lengthen it.

I'm going to assume that you're using your favourite chocolate, rather than pain au chocolat sticks. So put a strip of that, weighing around 30g, near to the end of the square. Fold over once, then add a second stick, near to the line where the fold meets the dough. Continue to fold, so that both sticks are completely enveloped in the dough.

Brush with egg wash – it gives a lovely colour and acts as a sealant, preventing the butter from running out of the dough as it cooks.

Bake at 230C for about 15 minutes, until golden brown.

Cool on a wire rack.

FRENCH FOLDING

ONCE you've mastered croissants, you'll be able to make myriad pastries.

You can add all sorts of fillings, from vanilla custard to dried fruits, or from apricot to chocolate. The secret is being able to fold.

There are numerous ways to fold laminated pastry, but I'm going to give you two examples which each follow a four-step process, and two more which are even quicker.

I'll start with an easy one, Turnovers. Then Windmills, which are easy and dramatic. You'll have fun making them.

Then Batman – so called because it looks like something the Caped Crusader might enjoy. It's pretty easy.

Then another simple one: Giants' Teeth.

TURNOVER

- Take a small square of laminated dough and fold it in half.
- Now take your plastic dough cutter and make incisions 1cm from the edge. Go all the way through the pastry. The incisions run from the folded-over edge, two thirds of the way up.
- Open out the square, by unfolding it and reversing the process in step one. Then take one outer corner and fold it over to join the small, inner square opposite. Repeat that action: bringing the outer corner over to touch the inner corner on the opposite side.
- Voila! You've completed a turnover.

WINDMILL

- Take a square of pastry and cut into each corner, towards the centre. Go through the pastry, two thirds of the way to the centre.
- Fold each corner to the centre.
- Repeat until you've folded each four corners.
- It was as easy as that.

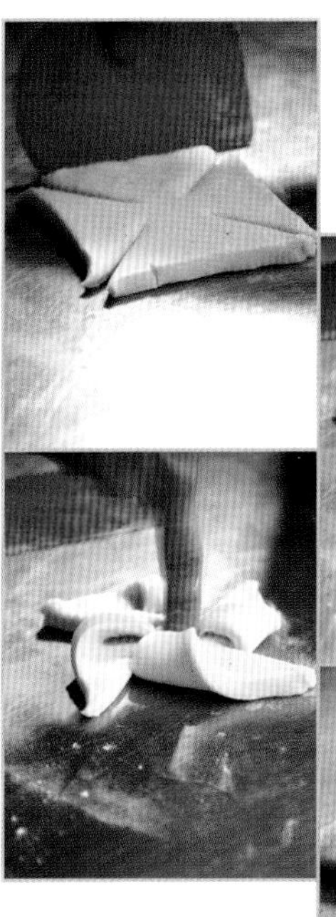

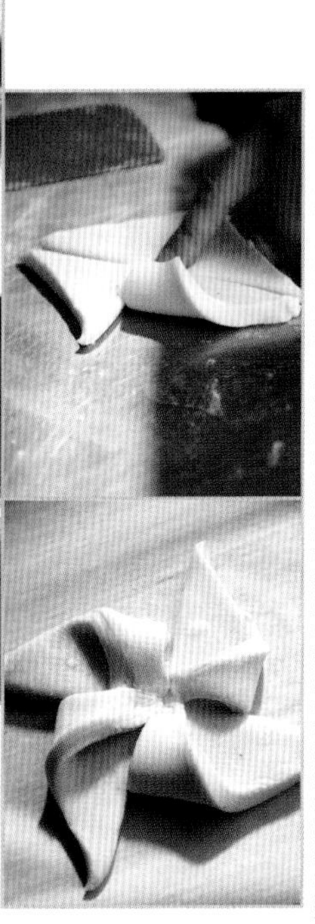

BATMAN

- Take a square of pastry and fold over, to make a triangle.
- On the long fold, make two incisions about five centres apart. They should be equidistance from the centre. Now pull down the 'wings'. It's Batman!

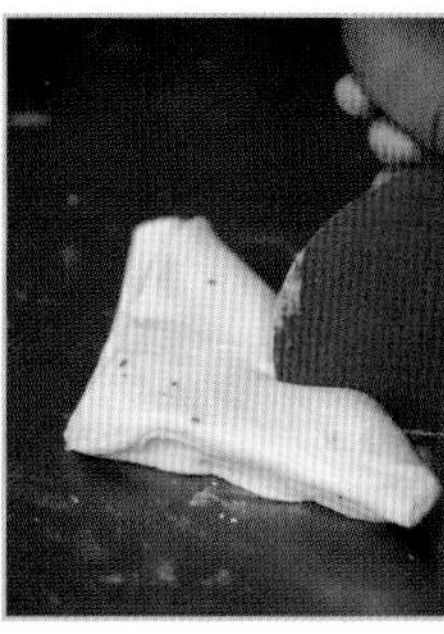

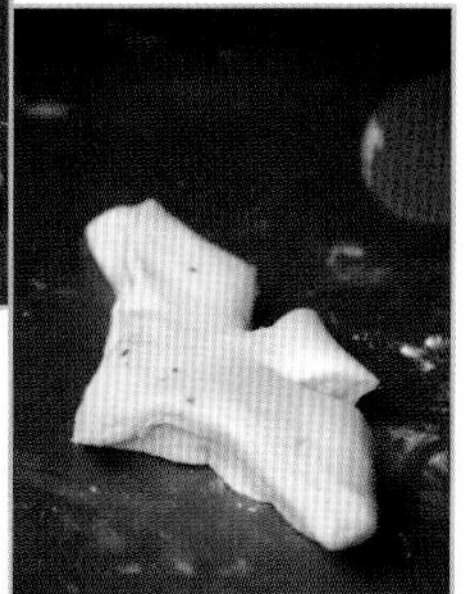

GIANTS' TEETH

- Take a square of pastry and fold over into an oblong. Then make a series of cuts 1cm apart, all the way along.
- Pull the sides out and round and that's it!

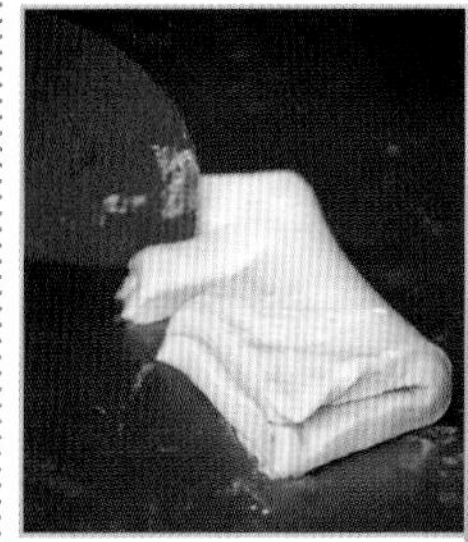

SHROPSHIRE BLUE AND RED ONION TWIST

THESE twists are real show-stoppers. They are relatively easy to make: you simply follow the same recipe that you would follow for a basic white loaf. Once you've completed your dough you apply a simple cut-and-fold technique, which gives it its 'twist'.

INGREDIENTS

500g French flour
340ml water
Extra water, up to 40ml, in accordance with the water method
8g salt
5g fresh yeast
Generous handful of Shropshire Blue cheese, grated
Half a red onion, finely sliced, and mixed into the cheese

Makes one large twist

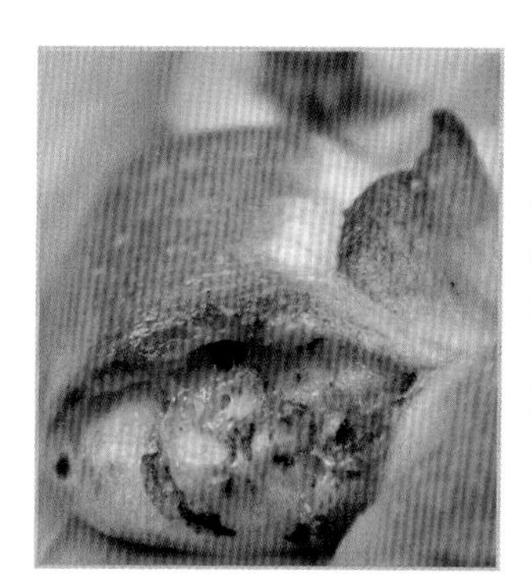

METHOD

Follow the instructions for making a basic white dough. So, combine your dry ingredients and set aside. Then add your yeast to the 340ml of water. Then slowly add the water and combine. Follow the water method and use all of the tests included in that section. Follow the kneading and resting process as you make your dough, giving it two rests of five or six minutes to achieve the desired gluten framework.

When it comes to fermentation, give the dough a two-hour rest. Turn and fold for 30 seconds, to release any gases, then give the dough its second rest, of between two and two-and-a-half hours.

Now take your dough and pin it out, using your fingers, into an A4 size. Butter the whole surface with melted, unsalted butter.

Now use your fingers the mark the dough into horizontal thirds, which will each have a maximum length of around 30cm. That creates tram lines, which are of an equal width. Now fill the centre with your cheese-and-red onion mixture. Do not go beyond the tramlines; if you do, you will be unable to roll it up.

Now fold the two ends over, so that the top corners are touching the bottom corners. You're making a big sausage roll shape. Press down and seal the dough ends together, using your fingers and thumbs.

When you are happy with your roll, it's time to make a series of cuts in the dough, which should be three-quarters of the way across. Make an incision through the dough every 5cm. Then complete your twist: simply roll one section over, then leave a section where it is. Now roll another section over, then leave the next section where it is. Repeat until you reach the end.

Leave to prove for a final 30–45 minutes and then bake at 230C, turning down to 220C after 10 minutes, for between 15 and 20 minutes: I always find 18 minutes works best.

bread2bake
enthusiasm, the perfect result!

Garlic and Herb Twist

THIS follows the same method and recipe as the Shropshire Blue and red onion twist, so I won't repeat the method here.

The only thing that changes, of course, is the filling. For this twist, I like to use one clove of fresh garlic, which should be finely chopped. If you are a fan of garlic, you can turn up the heat by adding another. I like the combination of parsley, coriander, thyme and chervil and I use a sprinkling of those four herbs.

INGREDIENTS

500g French flour
340ml water
8g salt
5g fresh yeast
1 clove of garlic
A handful of parsley, coriander, thyme and chervil

Makes one large twist

METHOD

Follow the instructions for making a basic white dough. Repeat the steps outlined on page 111 until you come to add your filling. Now fill the centre with your garlic and herb mixture.

Repeat the steps outlined on the previous pages; making your incision through the dough every 5cm and then folding over alternate sections.

Leave to prove for a final 30–45 minutes and then bake at 230C, turning down to 220C after 10 minutes, for between 15–20 minutes: I find 18 minutes works best.

TIP: You can vary the fillings if you wish. Another favourite of mine is mature Welsh cheddar cheese with leek. Apple and stilton also works well. There are myriad variations: be creative, use your imagination.

Pesto and Walnut Whirl

I COOK mine in a 15–16cm sponge tin when I bake these at home. I actually make four rolls in that size of tin with my 340g dough. However, when I'm doing them for the shop I make a large batch and cook them directly on the baking tray.

INGREDIENTS

125g white flour
125g '00' flour
160g water
4g salt
2g yeast
Half a jar of pesto
Generous handful of grated cheddar cheese
Half a handful of broken walnuts

You should have enough for between four and six whirls, depending on how hungry you're likely to be and how large you want to make them

METHOD

Follow the method for a basic white dough, giving the mix two rests of five or six minutes while you're making it.

When you reach the fermentation stage, give the dough a two-hour rest for the first rise, then fold and turn, before allowing a second rest of between two and two-and-a-half hours.

Once you've reached that stage, you can start to add your pesto and walnuts.

Firstly, lightly flour your working surface, then pin out the dough, using your hands, so that it is an A4-sized oblong.

Now take your pesto and cover the whole dough piece from end to end, top to bottom, on one side only. The covering of pesto should be even. Don't go mad, you still have to roll this up. Now sprinkle on a grated, nicely flavoured mature cheddar cheese. On top of that, spread the walnuts evenly over the dough piece.

Now start to fold. Take the top line of the dough and fold it over by an inch, then press it down into the dough. Roll it back, like you would a Swiss roll, but apply pressure as the dough meets the dough so that it's taut and the ingredients are kept in place. Roll it all the way over and press down to seal the dough at the bottom. Cut the rolled dough into four or five with a plastic cutter. Turn the five whirls so that they're standing up on their bottoms and you can see the rings inside. With the palm of your hand, slap them down – don't faff, be assertive and push them down. Now place them onto a baking tray or into a tin. Cover with a few more walnuts or a bit more cheese then prove for 30–45 minutes. They don't have to double in size, you're just looking for them to relax and start to move.

Bake at 230C, turning the oven down to 220C after 10 minutes. If you are baking them separately on a tray, cook for between 15–20 minutes – around 18 is best. If they are being baked together in a sponge tin, they'll be closer together so the baking time will increase. They'll probably take around 25 minutes, until the centre of the middle whirl is cooked.

Cheese and Tomato Whirl

THIS follows exactly the same recipe as the pesto and walnut whirl [*see page 115*]. Again, I favour cooking my own in a 15–16cm sponge tin, which means they have a very similar shape and have deliciously soft edges. You can play around with the shapes and sizes. If you want to serve these as a snack, cut them into much smaller pieces and they'll be absolutely delicious. Just remember to vary your baking times if you do so.

INGREDIENTS

125g white flour
125g '00' flour
160g water
4g salt
2g yeast
Generous handful of cheddar cheese, grated
Half a jar of sunblush tomato or tomato pesto

METHOD

Follow the same steps as you would for the pesto and walnut whirl.

The only difference is your filling.

Blitz your sunblush tomatoes and spread them over your dough piece. If you prefer, use a tomato pesto. You need to make sure you use a good melting cheese, such as cheddar. Avoid cheeses like Wensleydale or Cheshire, which don't melt as well.

Cook as described on page 111.

TIP: You don't have to stick to my choice of filling. Be as creating as you wish. Pick savoury flavour combinations that you like and let your imagination run riot!

LUDLOW
GREAT BEER, NATURALLY

LUDLOW BREWERY BEER BREAD

I'M a huge fan of great local food. I travel around the UK, attending food festivals and similar events, and the diversity of local produce is astonishing. In many ways, we are returning to the sort of food culture that Hannah Swift would have known, 150 years ago. Each town seems to have its own cheeses, ales, sausages and breads.

This recipe was inspired by a local brewery in Shropshire, the Ludlow Brewing Co, which serves a brilliant pint of real ale. I'd expect many of you to adapt it so that you can incorporate your own favourite pint into the recipe. The recipe can be made using one 500ml bottle of beer – what you don't use you get to drink. Cheers!

NOTE: This bread takes two days to make.

INGREDIENTS

FIRST MIX
200g white flour
10g sunflower seeds
10g sesame seeds
10g poppy seeds
10g pumpkin seeds
10g malted wheat flour
20g extratone malt
250ml beer (I use Ludlow Brewing Co's Black Knight, a 4.5 per cent stout with a ruby black complexion, a smoky, liquorice aroma and a sweet, roasted nutty flavour – though other beers can be used)

Makes one 2lb loaf or two 1lb loaves

METHOD

Work the dry ingredients together to form a dry mix, then add 250ml Black Knight stout – other beers are available. This needs to be done 24 hours before you make your dough.

➤

INGREDIENTS

SECOND MIX
200g white flour
50g wholemeal spelt
8g salt
6g yeast
120ml beer, at room temperature

METHOD

Take your 24-hour-old beer and flour mix, then begin to add your other ingredients. Start with the flours and salt. Set aside. Add your yeast to the beer, dissolve, then work into the flour. Follow the water method.

Once all of the yeasty beer has been added, complete your normal tests to make sure there is no dry flour. Spot in a little more beer if you need to. You are looking for nice tacky dough.

Give your dough two rests of five or six minutes during mixing. It will be difficult to complete the gluten window test, due to the high seed content. However, you should be able to ensure a good elasticity to your dough.

Once you are satisfied with your dough, cover and leave to prove for one-and-a-half to two hours. Turn and fold, then prove for a further two hours.

Divide the dough into two and use the 'bloomer' moulding technique. Wash with beer and add a sesame/poppy seed mix.

Place on baking tray and leave to prove for a final 45 minutes. Cut a criss-cross pattern on the top and bake immediately. Add steam to the oven using a spray bottle, and bake at 230C for 10 minutes, reducing to 220C for a further 30 minutes.

CHILLI, LIME AND CORIANDER BREAD

THIS is an intensely flavoured bread with a delightful, marbled appearance. It's important to marble the dough, rather than add the chilli to all of it. If you try to incorporate the chilli into the entire mix, you'll end up with a horrible, red-pink coloured loaf. You need lemon-and-lime oil for this, which you can make by steeping used lemons and lime in a jar of olive oil and leaving them to marinade.

INGREDIENTS

250g French flour
250g Italian '00' flour
340ml water
8g salt
5g yeast
1 tbsp of chilli paste
1 lime, zested and juiced
Handful of coriander
Lemon-and-lime oil
Handful of grated parmesan

Makes one 2lb loaf or two 1lb loaves

METHOD

Begin mixing in the normal way by adding flour and salt to a bowl and then mixing in the yeasty water. Now add in extra water, according to the water method. While the dough is still rough, add in the lime juice and continue to work. Spot in additional water, as required, until the dough becomes tacky. Do the pinch test to make sure the dough is good. The dough will be slightly different from a regulation white dough because the lime juice will have the effect of softening the gluten. Give the dough two rests of five or six minutes, while mixing.

Once the dough is mixed, cut it into four pieces. Place it back in the bowl and add your grated lime zest. Work that into the dough and rest for 90 minutes. Normally, at this point, you would turn and fold. However, on this occasion do not do that. Take your chilli paste and a metal scraper and cover the surface with a generous covering. Now cut through the dough and fold over; this action will create the marbling effect. Repeat several times, until you have marbled the dough. It will still be quite rough and messy, and needs to rest for a further 90 minutes. Then divide it into three even-sized pieces.

Oil a 15–16cm sponge tin with the citrus oil and place your dough into it; there is no need to mould. Prove for a further 30 minutes then bake at 230C for 20 minutes. Take it out of the oven and drizzle it with more citrus oil. Finish by grating a little parmesan over the top and some roughly chopped coriander.

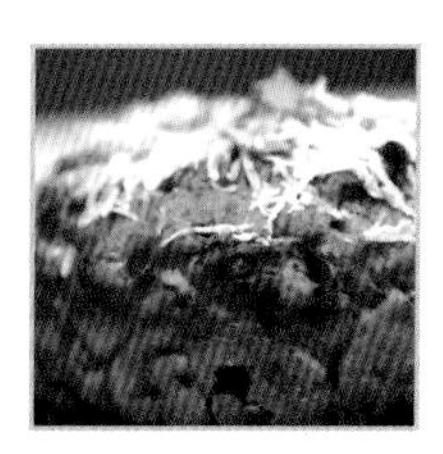

SCARBOROUGH FAIR

THIS loaf gets its name from a few of its ingredients: parsley, sage, rosemary and thyme. It's a wonderful loaf for slicing and eating with cooked meats or at dinner time. It contains potatoes, which are marinated for 24 hours before you bake. They add an intense flavour.

INGREDIENTS

FOR THE POTATOES
10 good-sized new potatoes
500ml olive oil
4 caps white wine vinegar
Juice of a lemon
3–4 cloves of garlic
Thyme, 5–6 sprigs
Rosemary, 4–5 sprigs

FOR MUSTARD SAUCE
150ml milk
10g cornflour
Knob of butter
2 heaped tsp grain mustard
¼ lemon, juiced
½ cap of white wine vinegar
Chopped parsley

FOR THE LOAF
250g tipo '00' flour
250g white flour
320g water
8g salt
5g yeast
6–8 sage leaves
Parsley, rosemary and thyme
Half a red onion, finely sliced

Makes two 'Fairs'

METHOD

Potato marinade. Twenty-four hours before you want to cook, make your marinade. Combine the olive oil, white wine vinegar and lemon juice, then add your garlic and herbs to the mix. Seal in a Kilner jar.

Boil your potatoes so that they are still firm in the middle and the starch is beginning to release. Slice them while still warm and then plunge into the marinade.

Mustard sauce. Place the cornflour in a saucepan and add a little milk, then start to work into a paste. Place the pan onto a medium heat and continue to stir, adding in the rest of the milk. Keep stirring until the sauce begins to thicken and then remove from the heat. Add the butter and melt through. Now, one by one, add the remainder of your ingredients, finishing with the parsley. The sauce will set as it starts to cool, if you don't use it straight away. If that happens, simply add a little olive oil to loosen it.

Loaf. Work together the dry ingredients, combine the water and yeast and then use the water method to create your dough, giving it two rests of five minutes. When you are happy and your dough has passed its checks, chop it into four pieces and place back in the bowl.

Chop the sage leaves finely, adding to the bowl and working into the dough. Bring the dough out onto the table to make sure they are evenly distributed. Place back into the bowl, cover and rest for 90 minutes, turn and fold before leaving for a further two hours. Now turn onto the table.

You can divide your dough into two equal pieces, each weighing approximately 430g. Then divide those into two and batch-mould them. Cover and rest for 10–15 minutes.

Once rested, take your first dough piece and begin to roll out with rolling pin into a 25cm circle. A little flour on the work surface will help: use the rolling pin a little and often to keep turning the dough.

Once you have divided your dough, place one piece on a baking tray. Using the scraper, add mustard sauce to your dough base, leaving a 4cm gap all around. Then take your potatoes and from the outside of the sauce lay the potatoes in a circle until you reach the centre. Take some red onion and sprinkle onto the potatoes. Finally take a little chopped rosemary and thyme and add.

When finished make another dough circle and spread a little sauce right in the middle; then take the disc and lay over the top of your filling, sauce side down. Go round with your fingers and thumbs and seal the edges of the two circles together. Take a pair of scissors and cut at a slight angle about 3cm into the dough around the edge of your circle at regular intervals. When you have gone all the way around, take each cut segment and fold over onto the next, to give a nice sealed 'Cornish pasty' edge.

Repeat the process for your second 'fair'.

Cover and prove for 30–45mins. Bake at 230C for 20–28 mins, then place on a cooling rack.

As soon as the bread is out, take some of the potato marinade and brush all over the bread. Allow to cool slightly, then sprinkle with chopped parsley.

WATERCRESS WINDMILL

A dramatic-looking bake!

INGREDIENTS

250g plain white flour
250g type '00' flour
340ml water
8g salt
5g yeast
20g parmesan cheese, finely grated
Watercress pesto

FOR THE WATERCRESS BUTTER
250G block unsalted butter
Generous handful of chopped watercress
1 shallot, finely chopped
1 clove garlic
30g ground almonds
Salt to taste

METHOD

First make your watercress butter. Soften the butter then mash it, so that it's falling apart but isn't melting. Add the remaining ingredients, then start to work it with a fork to combine them evenly. (If your butter is too soft when this is done, put it back in the fridge for 10 minutes to harden a little.)

Take a sheet of silicone paper or baking parchment that is larger than A4-size. Place the butter lengthways across the top third of the baking parchment and roll it over and over into a cylinder shape. Twist the ends, to make it taught, then freeze or refrigerate.

Now for the windmills. Use the tried and tested dough process, giving two five- or six-minute rests and applying the standard tests. Once you're happy with your dough, put it back into the bowl and chop into four pieces with your scraper.

Now add the parmesan cheese – this seasons the dough and gives texture and work it through the dough. Prove for 90 minutes, fold and turn, then give it another two hours proving.

Lightly dust a surface with semolina. Tip the dough out and with your fingers pin it out to an oblong about 5mm thick, then cut two equal square pieces. Lift one square onto a baking tray and spread the surface with a coating of pesto. Then from each corner, cut 5cm diagonally towards the centre. Take a corner on one side of each cut in turn, and fold into the middle, pressing the end down to keep it in place. You should end up with a shape like a child's toy windmill.

Prove for 30–45 minutes, then bake at 230C for 10 minutes, turning the oven down to 220 for a further 15 minutes.

Once cooked, take a slice of watercress butter the thickness of a one-pound coin and drop it onto the centre of the windmill to melt, then brush it out over the folded 'sails'.

TIP: If you don't use all the watercress butter in your baking, you can use it on pasta or potatoes.

Bagels

BAGELS are loved are around the world and can be eaten in myriad ways. They are thought to have originated in Krakow, Poland, more than 400 years ago. Today they are popular throughout Europe and the United States. Traditionally, they are eaten plain or topped with either sesame or poppy seeds, but there are literally hundreds of ways that they can be eaten. This basic recipe will get you started; after that, it's up to your imagination.

INGREDIENTS

500g flour
250ml water
8g yeast
6g salt
5g diastatic malt flour
5g sugar

Makes seven

METHOD

Make your dough following the usual method, being careful not to get the dough too wet. Our final dough will need to be firm yet smooth. Give the dough the normal tests, ensuring there is no dryness, then put to rest for two hours beneath oiled cling film.

Tip the dough onto the table and divide it into seven even pieces, which will each weigh around 120g. Using a 'roll' moulding technique, make them round and then cover and rest for a further 20 minutes.

At this point, place a large pan containing two litres of water on to boil and add six teaspoons of bicarbonate of soda. Get the water on a rolling boil. Now roll the dough pieces into sausage shapes roughly 15–18cm long, and squeeze the ends together to form a ring. Place them on a baking tray with silicone or parchment paper, which has been lightly oiled.

Place the bagels into the water, two at a time, boiling them for between 60 and 90 seconds each, until they have puffed up to double the size. Lift them out with a draining spoon and place back onto the tray, brushing with egg wash and sprinkling with poppy or sesame seeds, or even cheese.

Place the tray into the oven with a little steam: use your spray bottle for 10 seconds. Bake at 220C for 15 mins, turning down to 210C for a further five to eight minutes to finish.

Cider Bread

RATHER like my beer bread, this bake takes two days to make. It's worth the effort. The apple-y taste gives the loaf a real tang, which is ramped up by the use of rehydrated apple rings.

INGREDIENTS

Stage 1
100g white flour
100g wholemeal flour
50g rye flour
10g sesame seeds
10g poppy seeds
10g rolled oats
10g sunflower seeds
5g fennel seeds
250ml strong dry cider

Stage 2
8–10 dried apple rings

Stage 3
250g white flour
8g salt
5g yeast
3g sugar
100ml cider, plus extra as required
20ml water

Makes two 1lb loaves

METHOD

Stage 1. Mix the dry ingredients together and stir in the cider. Leave for 24 hours.

Stage 2. Soak the dried apple rings in cider overnight while the flour mix is fermenting.

Stage 3. Dissolve the yeast in the water – don't try to dissolve it in the cider, it will be too acidic. (More cider will be needed during mixing – and you'll probably need a drop to taste.)

This bread is put together in a very similar way to the beer bread, though it uses more sesame seeds, rolled oats and the wholemeal/rye flour. That makes it a thirsty mix, so be prepared to add quiet a lot of liquid to it. Even though we are not using water to hydrate the dough, we still want a soft dough.

Take your Stage 1 mix and add the flour, salt and sugar to the bowl. Add the yeasty water to the bowl. Work it together, then begin adding the cider and working it through. The 100ml will easily go in. Follow the water method (but using cider).

Bring the dough onto the table and begin to work it. Give it a minimum of two five-minute rests during mixing, though it may take three. Do the regular checks for smoothness and resistance. The gluten window tests could be undermined but the dough should remain nice and elastic. Divide the dough into four and place it back into the bowl. Chop your now-hydrated apples into little chunks and add. On the table, work the apple through the dough, making sure the apples are evenly dispersed. Pull together, place in a bowl and cover and prove for one-and-a-half to two hours. Turn and fold, then leave to prove for another two hours. Divide into two equal parts and mould either as 'batch' or 'bloomer'. Wash with cider and roll in flaked almonds.

Place on a baking tray and cover. Prove for 30–45 minutes. Bake at 220C for 25 minutes.

HONEY, MUSTARD AND DILL BREAD

THE flavours of this loaf sing out. The piquant heat of the mustard against the sweetness of the honey and aromatic savouriness of the dill make for an impressive loaf. Whoever thought that bread was all about sandwiches and toast ought to make this. Great flavours and a brilliant texture make it a standout bake.

INGREDIENTS

500g flour
340ml water
8g salt
8g yeast – a little extra yeast is needed to offset the honey and mustard
40g clear honey
80g mustard-and-dill paste, made by combining equal parts grain mustard and dill

METHOD

Work the dough using our tried-and-tested methods, by combining the dry ingredients and then adding in the yeasty water to take up the flour. The dough should be firm and a little on the dry/rough side. Do not hydrate your dough fully. When you have achieved a rough dough, work in the clear honey. It will form a sticky mix and you'll require plenty of effort. When the honey is fully incorporated, carry out your normal tests to make sure you've got a smooth dough.

Your dough may need a little more water, but be careful. While the dough should be tacky, you still need to work in your mustard-and-dill paste, which will add further moisture Put your dough on the table and begin to work as normal. Give it the usual rests and tests, then, when happy, cut it into four pieces and place it back into the bowl.

Add your mustard-and-dill paste and begin to work into the dough. When the paste has started to work into the dough bring it back to the table and work as before. You are looking to work all of the paste in so that it is no longer sticky. Cover and rest for two hours, then turn and fold. Rest for a further two hours.

Divide into two and use the batch mould and double mould. Place on a tray and cover. Prove for another hour, then cut and bake at 220–230C for 25–30 minutes. Mix a little honey and oil together and brush over your loaf.

SWEET BREADS AND CAKES

Basic Sweet Dough

SWEET doughs can be just as versatile as savoury doughs. They can be used to make butter buns, doughnuts, Chelsea buns, Belgian buns and many more besides. I've focused on a small selection that you'll be able to make with ease. You'll really impress your family and friends if you're able to make sweet treats for afternoon tea.

INGREDIENTS

700g white flour in total

First mix
- 280ml water, at 20–22C
- 35g sugar
- 25g yeast
- 15g milk powder
- Flour to thicken – 200–250g of the total 700g

Second mix
- Remainder of the flour – 450–500g
- 220ml water to start, more should be required using the water method
- 100g butter, unsalted
- 80g sugar
- 1 medium egg
- Juice of half a lemon
- 8g salt

METHOD

First mix. Dissolve the sugar, yeast and milk powder in the water, (which should be at 20–22C). Start adding your flour until it thickens to a paste. Allow this to ferment, doubling in size, then stir to knock down. Allow it to come again to the same size; your ferment is now ready to use.

Second mix. Take your ferment and add to the remainder of the flour in a mixing bowl. Soften the butter and add with the egg, sugar, salt and lemon juice. Add half of the water and begin to mix together. Use the water method to continue adding water.

The dough will be very soft because you have used butter and eggs. However, don't let that deceive you into leaving the water out. A lovely soft dough is what we're looking for, so persevere. Use the water method and give the dough three rests of between five and six minutes during mixing, before completing the usual tests. This dough will probably not sit up quite the same on the table as savoury dough. Place the dough in a bowl and cover. Prove for one hour, turn and fold, then prove for a further 90 minutes. Your final prove may be closer to an hour because the increased yeast content will reduce your proving time.

So, you've made your dough: what should you do now?

The dough you have created will allow you to make various sweet treats – or, as we would say, 'morning goods'. You'll be able to make Berlin doughnuts, Chelsea buns and Belgian buns, among many others. With the amount of dough this recipe gives you, you should be able to make an assortment of products. The following pages contain just a small selection of the things you could make.

BERLIN DOUGHNUTS

EVERYBODY loves doughnuts and Berlin doughnuts are the most popular of all. They are characterised by a pale line running around the middle of the doughnut. They should have a lovely golden colour on the top and on the bottom.

INGREDIENTS

300g sweet dough
Jam or other filling of choice
Caster sugar or vanilla sugar to coat

METHOD

To make these, you will need a deep fat fryer set at 180C. To make six doughnuts, take 300g and divide it into 50g pieces. You could make smaller doughnuts if you prefer, but I would not go below 25g each. Now mould using the 'rolls' technique to make little balls of dough.

Line a tray with baking parchment and flour it well. Place your doughnuts on the tray. Space them out to allow them to double in size. Cover and allow them to prove for approximately one hour.

Make sure your fryer is at the correct temperature then carefully place two or three doughnuts into the fat. It should bubble a lot when your doughnut hits it. Once the bubbles begin to subside the doughnut is ready to turn. Use a draining spoon to do that by just pushing down on one side and flipping over. Once the doughnut is fried, lift it out onto a cooling rack with paper beneath to catch the oil.

Once they have cooled a little use a skewer or a corkscrew and push that into the side of doughnut. You'll then be able to pipe jam or apple filling or even custard into the side, using a piping bag and nozzle. Just gently push in, squeeze and pull out as you do.

Once your doughnuts are filled, roll them in caster sugar or vanilla sugar. Serve and enjoy.

Chelsea Buns

CHELSEAS are the upper crust buns. They were favoured by Hanoverian royalty and were first created in the 18th century in Chelsea, at Bun House. Once you've mastered Chelsea buns, you'll be able to expand your repertoire and make cinnamon rolls, which are produced using a very similar process.

INGREDIENTS

680g sweet dough
140g currants or raisins
Large knob of unsalted butter, melted
2 tbsp granulated sugar
1 tsp cinnamon or mixed spice

For sweet glaze
500ml water
200g sugar
5 tsp lemon curd

METHOD

Lightly flour your table. Roll the dough out using a rolling pin into a rectangle shape. It should be a little smaller than A4-sized and no thinner than 1cm. Brush your dough with melted butter, then spread over the currants or raisins. Spread top to bottom, left to right, ensuring an even coating. Then take your sugar, mixed with the spice, and sprinkle over the top. (Don't overdo it: too much sugar and spice could retard our final proof.)

Begin to roll up from top to bottom to make a Swiss roll (see the Stromboli/Pesto Whirl recipes, for details). When rolled, brush with more melted butter and mark off at 2.5cm intervals along the dough, cut through and then lay the slices on a lined baking tray. Do this butter-side to none-butter side. You will only require a small gap between each roll as you want them to stick together. Prove for 45–60 minutes, until the tray is full of dough. Bake at 230C for 10–12 minutes, checking after 10 minutes and turning down to 220C. Take out and cool.

Prepare your glaze. Heat the water, sugar and lemon curd in a pan. Bring to the boil, turn down and simmer for three or four minutes. While still hot, brush over your Chelseas and then sprinkle with more of the sugar you used in the centre. Forget about the calories and enjoy.

Belgian Buns

THESE are produce in a similar way to Chelseas, with just a couple of changes. Use brown sugar instead of granulated sugar and do not add any cinnamon or spice. Use sultanas instead of currants and add a few chopped cherries, and 10g of mixed peel. Roll up and cut in exactly the same way but when traying-up, leaving a 5cm gap between them. Prove and bake in the same way. Cut down the baking time to eight to 10 minutes. Use sugar lemon wash and a little fondant icing in the middle.

Iced Rolls and Fingers

THESE are very similar to Berlin doughnuts and need to be weighed and moulded in the same way. Of course, if you choose fingers, instead of rolls, the moulding process will differ.

This is what to do for fingers: rather than leave them round, roll the dough out to roughly 15cm long finger-roll shapes. Line your tray with baking parchment or silicone paper and line the rolls up on it, leaving enough room for them to double in size without touching. Cover and prove for one hour. Bake at 230C for eight to 10 minutes. Bake to colour, looking for a pale golden shade. Always check the buns after eight minutes because they colour quickly due to the high sugar content.

Once baked, leave to cool. Soften fondant icing and dip the roll into the icing. Remove any excess by moving the roll up and down. Place on a rack and allow to dry. They are great for kids' parties or enjoyed with a cup of tea in the afternoon.

CHEESECAKES

THIS recipe makes cheesecakes that are unrecognisable from the standard digestive plus butter, with a Philly-and-cream topping. Give it a go. You need food rings to form their circular shape.

INGREDIENTS

50g amaretti biscuits
50g ginger nuts
50g unsalted butter, melted
150ml double cream
250g mascarpone cheese
½ vanilla pod
60g brown caster sugar
Fruit to flavour

Makes 4 cheesecakes

METHOD

Place the biscuits in a bag and use a rolling pin to break them up. Don't make them too fine, they are better if a little rough with non-uniform sizes. Place the crushed biscuits into a bowl and add the melted butter, mixing until all the biscuits are coated with the butter.

Place your food rings on a tray and begin to fill each ring with the biscuit. Each ring should take a couple of tablespoons and you are looking for a thickness of no less than 1cm. Once the mixture is in, use the back of a teaspoon or your thumb to push it down. Firm the base and make it as even as possible. Place in the freezer to set for 15–20 minutes.

For the filling you will need two mixing bowls.

Weigh the mascarpone into one bowl and with a wooden spoon beat it until it becomes soft and smooth. Add the sugar and combine. Slice open the vanilla pod and add the contents to the cheese and sugar, and combine. (Don't throw away the empty pod, place it a bag with some sugar to create delicious vanilla sugar, which you can use another day.)

Whisk the double cream in the other bowl until it reaches soft peaks. Then add your cream to the mascarpone mix. Gently work together.

To flavour, roughly chop fruit – strawberries or raspberries are good – and place them into a bowl. Six good size strawberries is enough; eight or 10 raspberries. Gently work them into the mix, then take a matching, high-fruit jam and add two or three teaspoons to the mix. Fold in so that it has a marbled effect.

To assemble, fill half of the ring with the mixture, pushing down as best as you can. Add a teaspoon of jam in the middle, then spoon more filling on top. Fill it just beyond the ring, then with a blunt straight edge remove the excess to leave an even surface. Place in fridge or freezer to set. They will keep for two or three days. Bring out 45 minutes before serving to allow them to thaw. After 15–20 minutes, push the cheesecakes from the bottom and remove from the rings.

Ronde des Pains
Cherry
Tomato

FESTIVALS AND MARKETS

IT'S remarkable how things come full circle. A century-and-a-half ago, bakers would have made bread for market day, as well as selling from the shop. People would have travelled into their local towns to buy their weekly food.

During the past decade or so, a similar pattern has emerged.

Ludlow has been at the vanguard in terms of both markets and festivals. The Ludlow Food Festival was launched in 1994 when a group of local businessmen wanted to combat the threat posed by supermarkets to the town's independent stores. They reasoned that an annual celebration of great local food would shine the spotlight on the small producers who were creating 'real' food using traditional methods.

It worked, and now the Ludlow Food Festival has been copied up and down the country by towns that stage similar events. We get involved in scores of them, taking our breads around the country to people who are passionate about real food.

I frequently demonstrate at those events, trying to come up with new and exciting ways of getting people involved. Whether it's showing people the basics, like making a wholemeal loaf, or offering tips on how to make something more creative, such as ice-cream cones, they leave the audience thrilled.

We're regulars at markets, too, travelling along the highways and byways most weekends to sell in Nottingham, Shrewsbury or further afield. The lion's share of the markets are run very succesfully by Jayne and John (when he can); this year alone they have organised at least 50 festivals and markets. Their efforts allow us to be in more than one place at any given time!

The markets present a chance for us to go back to our roots. We're no longer bogged down in administration or accounting; we're able to bake early in the morning, load our vans and then sell to people who love great food.

The markets and festivals also give us the chance to introduce the sixth generation of Swifts to our business. My two sons are regulars at markets, joining their grandparents on Sunday mornings. They thoroughly enjoy the interaction with the crowds and love telling people about our long and proud heritage.

Festivals and markets are our way of telling more people about the virtues of great, artisanal food. Who knows, I may see you on the road someday soon.

Robert Swift demonstrating at Ludlow Food Festival, 2013.

Schools and WI

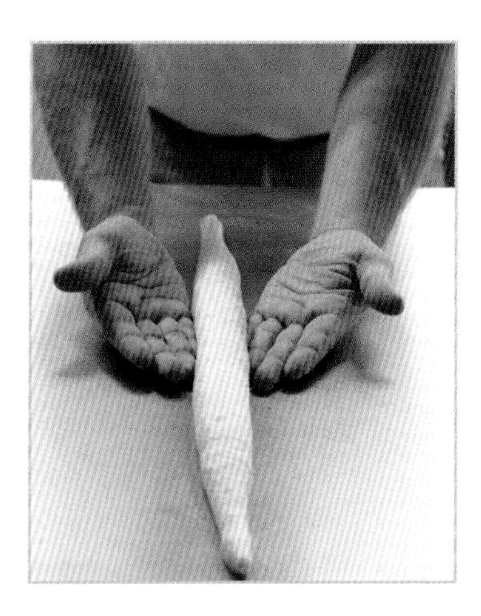

THERE was a time, not so long ago, when cooking was considered 'sissy'. The only people who'd sign up for cooking or baking lessons at school were girls. Boys would be out playing football or rugby, they wouldn't dream of going inside a home economics classroom.

That's all changed, thankfully, and now both sexes realise the importance of being able to cook and bake. In Ludlow, which has a vibrant food community, food lessons are not just enjoyable, they're also cool.

Senior schools nearby run an excellent programme called Skillbuilders, which encourages the younger generation to learn food skills. They take to their lessons with gusto, learning how to bake simple breads and progressing swiftly to more complicated bakes.

A small number of artisans, including bakers, chefs and other producers, take part in the Skillbuilders programme on a voluntary basis.

We go into our local schools and teach children about the importance of great, local food that is produced with love and affection. They thoroughly enjoy it.

As a tutor, I get enormous pleasure from passing on my skills to youngsters. Seeing their faces light up as they bake their first loaf is a true privilege. I know that I am passing on skills that will last a lifetime. After all, that has been my experience. Five generations of my family have passed their skills down to me, with my father, Richard, teaching me as a young boy.

And now, through Skillbuilders, I get to do the same. I thoroughly enjoy taking part in those sessions and I've no doubt that some of the children who I teach will go on to have careers in food.

It's not just the younger generation that we reach out to. I also run a busy programme working with local Women's Institute groups. They are great fun. The ladies who attend such groups have considerable knowledge, having baked for many years.

They constantly challenge my methods and seek explanation – and usually accept that I know what I'm doing. They are spirited, knowledgeable, attentive and keen to learn.

Being part of the community in Ludlow, Tenbury Wells and other parts of Shropshire and Worcestershire is a real joy.

Courses

SWIFT'S may well have celebrated 150 years of history in 2013 – but time does not stand still.

Throughout our family's history, we have continued to innovate. My forebears sought new ways to bring freshly baked bread to market, opened shops in different towns, created new products and forever maintained the highest possible standards.

My own business, Bread2Bake, is an extension of that. I offer a variety of breadmaking courses and the take-up has been phenomenal.

There has been a resurgence of interest in 'real' food during the past decade or so. People are no longer prepared to put up with the shelf-filling, mass-produced, flavourless products that fill the aisles of many of our supermarkets. They are looking for something different, something better. And that, happily, is where we come in.

Swift's has always striven to be the best. We've looked to create bakes that people can trust and enjoy. We run a family business and my father, my brother and I all strive to innovate. We are never content to rest on our laurels; we're always pushing to improve.

Bread2Bake is part of that yearning to be the best.

The upswing in interest for artisan food has been accompanied by an interest among people who want to make their own produce at home. That is why I began a series of courses here in Ludlow.

We opened a new bakehouse, at 135 Corve Street, and it contains a room that we use to tutor our students. It has proved a hit: who knows, one day soon we might be forced to seek larger premises.

The courses are a joy because they take place in the same bakery that is used to supply a lot of the goods for our shop. We run one-day courses and two-day courses that focus on particular areas of interest. I also conduct courses elsewhere, for instance, at Brompton Cookery School, near Shrewsbury, which is owned and operated by the chef Marcus Bean.

Here at our headquarters, we focus on a variety of different elements: many of which are featured in the pages of *Born & Bread*.

On our introductory course, we explore both machine- and hand-mixing, the use of different flours and different methods of fermentation. Is this starting to sound familiar?

We also look at the creation of poolish and sourdough and at ways of incorporating different flavours into breads – for instance, by using vegetables, herbs, pestos or sauces. We're always open to new ideas and the happiest times come when students give me new ideas – while I'm happy to teach people, I'm just as happy to learn new ideas.

Those attending a course mix at least one dough during the day, moulding it and shaping it themselves. That may be a tin loaf, small individual rolls, a single-strand plait, knots or even a hedgehog. If there's time, we create speciality breads using French and Italian flours.

There is always plenty of time for people to ask questions. There are other speciality courses, which focus on French and Italian bakes. We produce such breads as focaccia, ciabatta, Stromboli and grissini on the Italian course. On the French course, we make croissants, baguettes, rustic loaves or brioche. Again, these will incorporate both machine- and handmade methods.

We explore advanced methods of breadmaking, with longer, overnight fermentations. We also look at a variety of moulding techniques and explain how they can affect your final loaves. We have plenty of

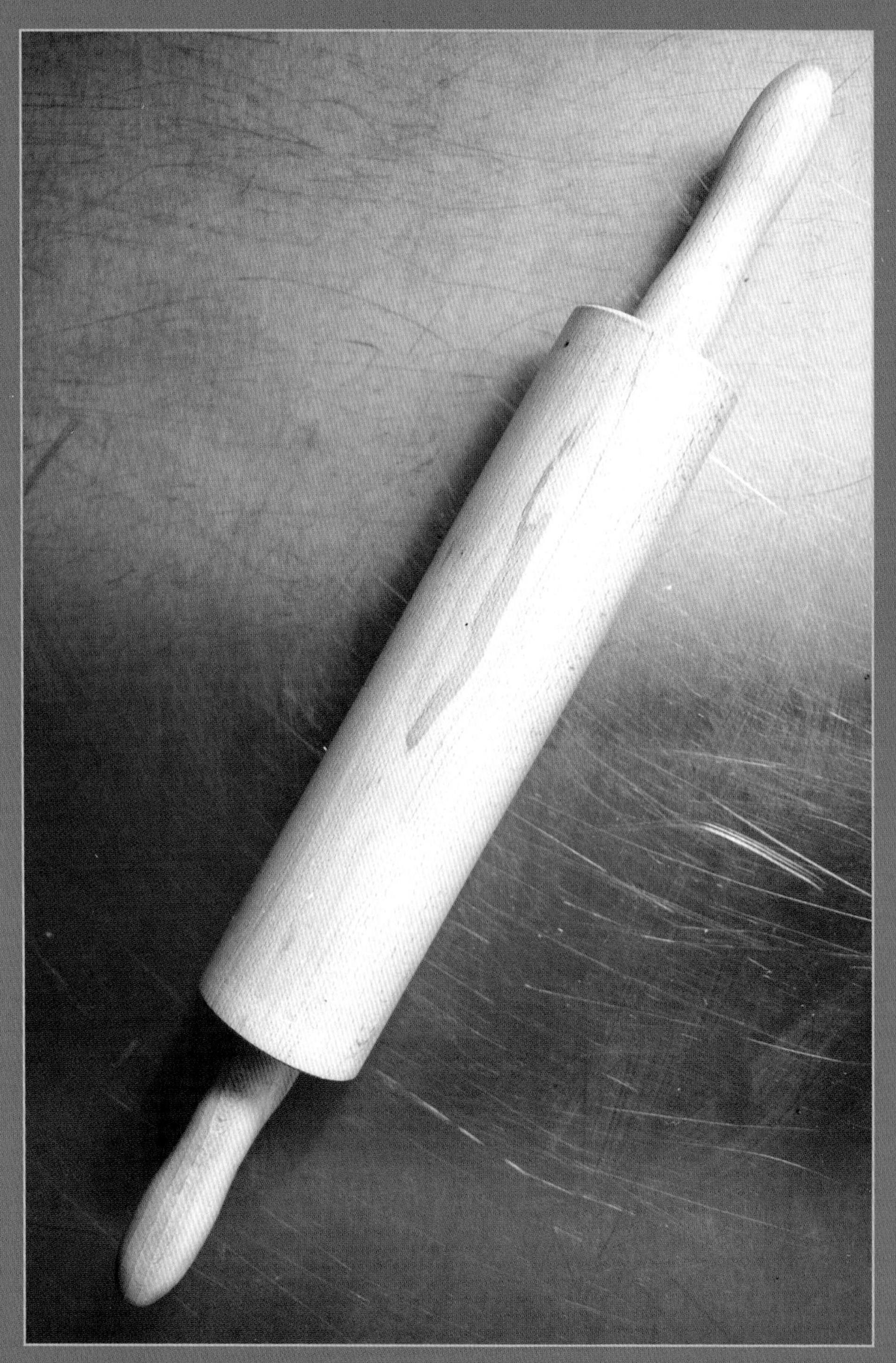

chance to practice and then create speciality breads.

As tutor, I am always thrilled when my students do well. The objective is for people to learn in an environment that is relaxed, fun and informative. Baking has become increasingly fashionable in recent times and it's great to be part of a new wave. People no longer want the same old thing from their local supermarket; they either want to buy a quality product or they want to make one of their own.

Here at Swift's, we try to achieve that through our shops and through our Bread2Bake courses.

We're always open to new ideas and if people have a particular interest in a certain type of baking, they are more than welcome to ask me for details.

Hopefully, *Born & Bread* will give you an appetite for home baking. And – if you've not already attended one of our Bread2Bake courses – this book might persuade you to get in touch.

● **Further details are available at www.bread2bake.co.uk**

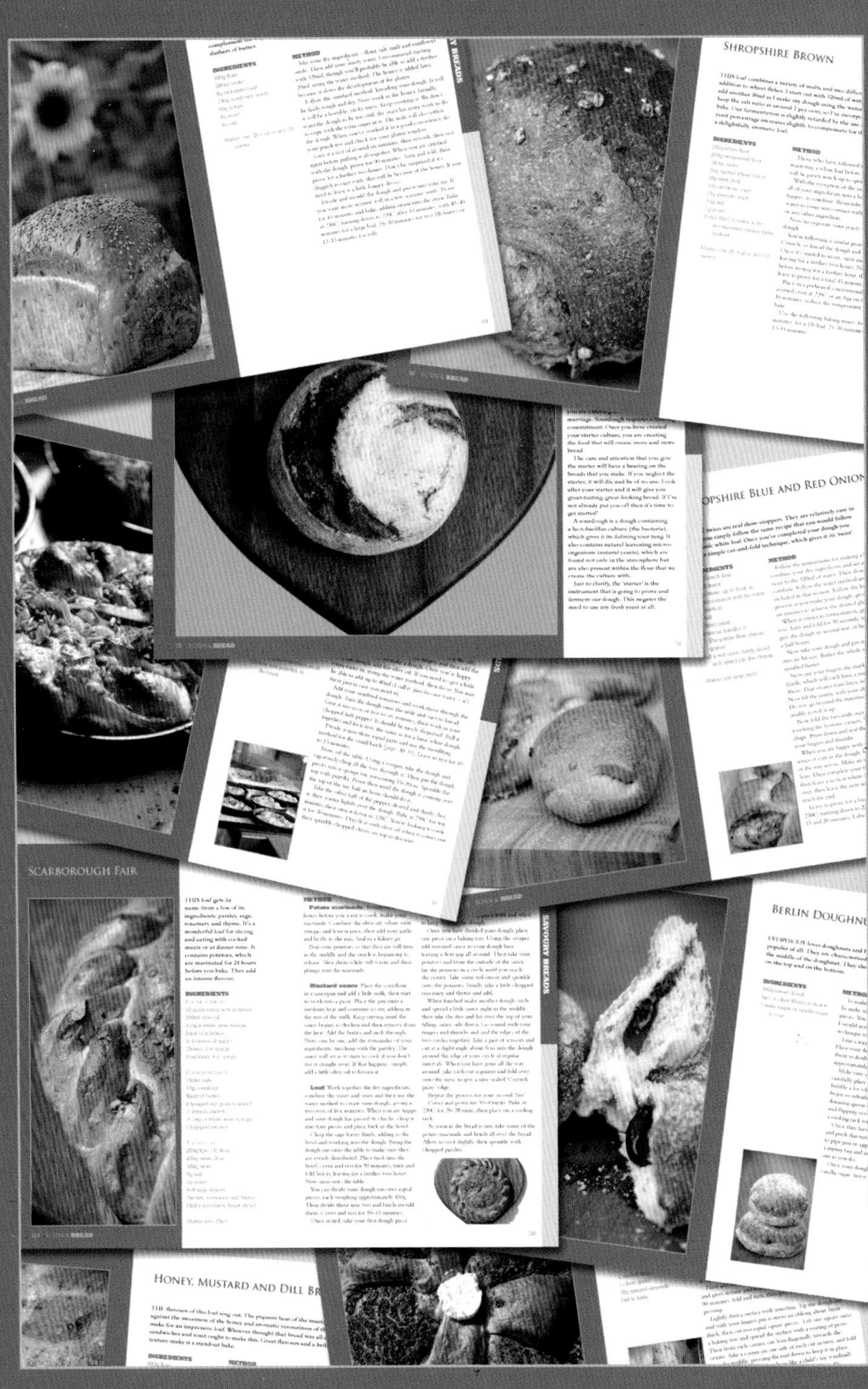
Shropshire Brown
Scarborough Fair
SAVOURY BREADS

INDEX

Acknowledgements

A LOT of the people that I need to say thank you to are unfortunately not with us anymore. I am of course talking about Hannah, Harriet and all those who were involved in the making of the Swift family business. I didn't have the opportunity to meet these people but without them there wouldn't have been a Swift family baking tradition for 150 years now.

I did, however, have the privilege of knowing, learning and working with my Granddad. He was a no-nonsense individual, who cared deeply about the breads that he made. He instilled that sense of pride in all of us: my father, my brother and I. We all wish both he and Grandma were here to celebrate our 150th anniversary and the publication of our book.

A big thank-you must go to my mum and dad, too, who have worked endlessly and with great determination to create a business for John and I. We intend to continue the family tradition. Dad is a constant inspiration, who won't let anything beat him. And mum is the glue that binds us all. She is a truly amazing woman and has done every job in the bakery, shop and on the van.

A big thank-you also goes to my brother John and his wife Jayne for everything that they do. They work long and hard for the family. John shows the same determination and passion that my Granddad had: those qualities are among the reasons why I love him.

I'm grateful to my own sons, Elliott and Mackenzie, for just being themselves and understanding that the hours I put in at work often takes me away from them – unless there is a Leeds United match.

My dear wife, Luci, has been a font of inspiration, particularly for this project. She has been steadfast and encouraging throughout. She has been my rock. She understands the life of a baker and never protests or stands in my way. I'd like to thank her from the bottom of my heart, for not only helping me but helping us.

I'd also like to thank our staff – without them, we'd have no business.

I'm grateful to Brompton Cookery School owner Marcus Bean for writing a foreword. It's a privilege to know him and his beautiful family.

I'm indebted to designer Adam Haynes for making *Born & Bread* look every bit as good as I had imagined. He has artfully captured the essence of what we had envisioned.

And finally, I'd like to thank Andy Richardson, who works longer hours than a baker and whom it has been a pleasure to get to know.

ROBERT SWIFT, *Ludlow, 2013*

E
W

WWW.BREAD2BAKE.CO.UK